"THE GOD PLOT"

by
TIMOTHY M. GREEN

Living with Holy Imagination...

BEACON HILL PRESS
OF KANSAS CITY

To my mother,
Delores Green,
whose steadfast faith, courageous hope,
and self-giving love
have exemplified the godly life.
Your children rise up and call you blessed.

CONTENTS

PREFACE
ONE MORE CLICHÉ

AFTER the book of Ecclesiastes declares "What has been is what will be, and what has been done is what will be done; there is nothing new under the sun" (1:9), it concludes with an ever-so-true statement: "Of making many books there is no end, and much study is a weariness of the flesh" (12:12). I would never have the audacity to suggest that the material within this book is new. There is so much printed material and social media available today that I am respectfully aware that this book simply adds one more voice to the "making of many books" to which "there is no end." However, it is my hope and prayer that this book will provide an enlivened and fresh vision of God's great story. It is in this story—this God plot—that God calls his people and ultimately all of humanity to participate. My deep desire is that this book will result in a renewed call upon the people of God across geographical, linguistic, and traditional lines to live beyond the familiar clichés and code words that we create and on which we often unthinkingly base our lives. I have no desire to rid our vocabulary of those code words, but I pray that they will be filled with such deep, broad, and wide meaning that we will once again come to recognize and celebrate that God desires to "accomplish abundantly far more than all we can ask or imagine" in the lives of his people (Eph. 3:20).

This book is the result of over a decade and a half of interaction with some of the finest followers of Jesus Christ across the world. Beginning with a morning Bible study in West Texas, I responded to an invitation at a summer family camp to include with my evening and morning sermons a small-group study on biblical holiness. Over the next few years, that Bible study expanded as I traveled throughout the country from one summer family camp to another.

While I was enthralled by the insights I was gleaning as the dots in the overarching narrative of Scripture began to connect in my mind, I was equally fascinated by the number of people, both clergy and lay, who would forgo additional rest during the lazy months of summer and come to the study during the early morning hours. I began to realize that there was indeed a hunger and thirst for Bible study that approaches the Bible as a whole instead of only looking at its most minute parts. People were interested in the theological realities that find their bases in Christian Scripture and the historical Christian tradition; they wanted to understand the biblical and theological truths that intersect the real world of their lives. I began to recognize that people desired more than familiar clichés and code words that may have begun well but somewhere along the way became emptied of their meaning. I also began to celebrate the biblical reality of what I myself had over time diluted to code words and propositional statements: God calls his covenant people to undivided fidelity and trust in him, and the God who calls his people is faithful, and he himself will do what he promises.

Along the way, my fascination in the Bible studies at summer family camps led to the joy and privilege of sharing in various lecture series on university campuses. Special thanks go to Southern Nazarene University, Mount Vernon Nazarene University, and Olivet Nazarene University for inviting me to be the guest lecturer at their annual holiness lecture series. In time, I had the special joy of translating much of what was developing in my mind from a North American context into an Eastern European context by instructing an outstanding group of students in Sofia, Bulgaria. It was a special joy to fine-tune much of what I had discovered in my biblical journey by teaching a graduate seminar twice on holiness in the Old Testament at the academic institution I have called home for almost twenty-five years, Trevecca Nazarene University. Then finally, it was a privilege to share much of this material for two days in Denver with a group of over fifty of the most dedicated ministerial administrators at their district superintendents leadership conference; their passion that the God plot be delivered to the people of God with biblical, theological, and practical integrity inspired my own passion all the more.

It has been an amazing journey, and it all began when my own eyes were suddenly opened and I recognized that what God is doing in his world is so much bigger than a good cliché or a well-memorized propositional statement. The dots of the biblical God plot connect! People of all ages, intellectual levels, and cultural and ethnic backgrounds—both lay and clergy—hunger and thirst to hear, to receive, and to embody the God plot. To the end of nourishing this hunger and thirst by the grace of God through the work of his Holy Spirit, I modestly provide one more book to the many that have been and will be written. My prayer is especially that preachers and teachers of the Bible will have a renewed awareness that the divine invitation to holiness, to unadulterated loyalty, to the undivided love of God and love of neighbor, is legitimate and authentic. My prayer is also that those same preachers and teachers will be touched with a fresh spark of holy imagination so that they can both read Scripture and communicate it with holy imagination. I offer this prayer in the context of the following blessing upon all those who will teach and preach the God plot to present and future generations:

> May the God of peace himself sanctify you entirely; and may your spirit and soul and body be kept sound and blameless at the coming of our Lord Jesus Christ. The one who calls you is faithful, and he will do this. (1 Thess. 5:23-24)

INTRODUCTION
DISCOVERING THE GOD PLOT

"BAD HAIR DAY," "dirt cheap," "eat crow," "smoking gun," "to each his own"—we hear them and use them every day at every turn. They are clichés, code words, and catch-phrases that take on lives of their own. They tell stories in themselves. Every language and culture has them. We so easily become enculturated into them that we throw them around without even thinking about what they actually mean. In fact, they often lose their meanings entirely.

Isn't it amazing? In the opening sentences of this introduction, at least three of them have already occurred: "every turn," "lives of their own," "throw them around." They are so common to our thinking and speaking that if someone were to stop us in the middle of a sentence and ask us to explain a cliché we just used, we would likely become startled and perhaps be at a loss for words.

It seems to happen in every area of our lives. We become enculturated into the language, even the mannerisms, of our families, our societies, and the different groups to which we belong. We usually learn these code words and catchphrases before we ever learn their meanings. Do you remember those vocabulary tests growing up? You had heard and spoken the words for years. You often even knew how to use them appropriately in a sentence because you were mimicking all the times you had heard your parents, siblings, friends, and teachers use them. It's just the way culture and language work; however, then came the vocabulary test. You actually had to explain what those familiar words meant. It was difficult enough to memorize a formal definition, but the real test came when you had to reuse the word appropriately in a sentence or describe its meaning in a particular sentence.

Often certain code words become labels for interpreting the thoughts and actions of specific individuals or groups of people. The words tell the story: "conservative," "liberal," "Gen X," "Gen Y," "modern," "postmodern," "mainstream," "third world," "white collar," "blue collar," "believer," "nonbeliever," and so on. They paint a black-and-white picture (how is that phrase for one more cliché?) by which we can define people from the closest family member to a total stranger. But once again, when pushed for a definition, we might struggle to articulate exactly what we mean by a code word that has classified another person.

Because the use of these clichés and catchphrases is a part of every aspect of our lives, it comes as no surprise that followers of Jesus Christ find themselves hearing, speaking, and writing their own set of clichés. Just think about the catchphrases and code words that followers of Jesus hear and use. We insert them over and over again into our songs, we hear them in sermons and Bible studies, and we utter them in our prayers. Our parents and grandparents used them in such a natural way that it was almost as if they didn't even have to think about them. As they got older, they simply enculturated us to use those catchphrases and code words in our vocabulary. Now as we get older, we simply do the same with the next generation. This is just the way culture and language work, including the culture and language of the people of God.

Think about just a few of those code words: "saved," "forgiven," "called," "grace," "faith," "holiness," "God's Word," "justice," "discipleship," "commitment," "righteousness," and "love." Okay, now don't get me wrong. These words and many others like them are beautiful gifts that we have inherited. Usually they arise from Christian Scripture and have been handed down through the generations by faithful men and women in order to communicate the most remarkable realities that the human mind can ever imagine. At times this language is expressed in spoken words. At other times it is expressed through silent symbolic acts.

This common language that we use with each other and that one generation passes on to the next generation is our Christian culture's primary means of communicating and dependably transmitting the faith. At times the language serves as an unbroken bridge to past and future generations. At other times, the language remains the same, but the words and clichés evolve in their meanings from one generation to the next. Still at other times, subsequent generations create their own code words for the season in which they find themselves living.

While this language filled with code words and symbolic actions is a great gift, it also presents each generation a great dilemma! As words are removed from their larger contexts, they can have a variety of meanings or even become meaningless. We understand words only within their contexts. For example, think about the word "safe." In the three statements below, notice how the context determines the meaning of each appearance of the word:

- I plan to lock up the jewels in the bank's safe.
- The first-base umpire cried out, "Safe!"
- After the storm, everyone in the house was safe.

Now if even a sentence can make such a difference in the meaning of a word, just think about the difference that a full paragraph can make in the meaning of a sentence. Imagine the difference that a book in its totality can make in the meaning of a single chapter or the difference that a full song can make in the meaning of a single verse.

Hearing the Code Words and Clichés within the Larger Story: Engaging in the God Plot

Although many of the tightly held clichés, code words, symbolic acts, and catchphrases that the people of God have inherited and use today are beautiful and good, what if over time they have become so separated from the overarching story of God that they have lost their original meanings? What if valued words and phrases that once held deep and profound significance have unwittingly been lifted out of the grand plot of God and have been dropped into our sermons, our Bible studies, our songs, and our prayers. What if we continue to carry out the actions and to sing, pray, and preach the words that—now separated from their context— are empty of the profound importance of what God is doing and longing to do in the life of his people and in the world? What if the statement made by twentieth-century philosopher Ludwig Wittgenstein speaks to our own use of favorite catchphrases and clichés: "A picture held us captive. And we could not get outside it, for it lay in our language and language seemed to repeat it to us inexorably."[1]

There is a particular set of words and clichés that seem to drop easily out of the context of the God plot and yet drop back into the language of our songs, prayers, and sermons. These code words and their accompanying acts seem to repeat themselves again and again, and we seem trapped in their continual but often empty use. They are perhaps some of the most popular words and clichés in the Christian faith, but they hold us "captive" and we cannot "get outside" them. No matter what our Christian affiliation or heritage or our historical era or geographical location, these catchwords and the symbolic actions associated with them repeat themselves to us "inexorably." Of all the vocabulary of the Christian journey, there's probably none more cliché filled than the language associated with holiness.

Think about some of the code words Christians have used and continue to use to converse about holiness: "holy" ("holiness"/"make holy"/"unholy"), "perfect," "whole," "complete," "sanctify" ("sanctified"/"sanctification"), "purity" ("purify"/"pure"/"impure"), "cleanse"/"wash" ("clean"/"make clean"/"unclean"). It seems that every corner of the Christian faith uses this language in one way or another, often placing it in diverse contexts that give it diverse meanings. We use it to speak about God and God's character, but we also use it to speak about ourselves and our character. Sometimes we use it in the negative ("We are not holy [unholy]"), sometimes we use it in the positive ("We are holy"), and sometimes we use it in the realm of possibilities ("God calls us to be holy").

If what these code words and clichés and their accompanying rituals represent were not so central to what God is doing in the life of his people, the world, and all creation, then everything we have just said would be a mere curiosity of language, a game about culture. But if what these words and phrases represent is the focal point of what God is doing in the world, particularly in relationship to his covenant people, then we probably should stop the language game, take a deep breath, and reread and rehear the story of God's work in the world and the story of his imagination and hope for the world.

To find ourselves in the story line of God—the God plot—by no means requires us to cast off the clichés, to dispose of the familiar language, or to abandon the accompanying symbolic actions. However, to engage in the God plot with holy imagination is to return to the scheme of God as rehearsed in Sacred Scripture and as embodied in centuries of the Christian faith. A firmly held conviction informs all of our discussion that follows: while our clichés are often based on good, solid words, phrases, and symbolic acts that have often emerged out of Scripture and out of the grand Christian tradition, God is into something so much more than a checklist of catchphrases, propositions, and their accompanying actions. Code words all too easily become flat; clichés, empty; propositional statements, void of meaning; and accompanying symbolic acts, hollow. In spite of the best intentions, they can finally fall on deaf ears or misunderstanding minds.

While it may at first appear important to rid ourselves of popular clichés, tightly held catchphrases, and accompanying symbolic acts, that is not the issue at hand. The dilemma we most often face is not in the words and actions themselves but in their being lifted *out of* the overarching story of God, refilled with separate meanings all their own, and left as ends in themselves—isolated from the God plot.

In contrast to their wholesale abandonment, dull and gray clichés can reappear with an enlivened vibrancy and animated vigor when they are placed back in the brilliant context of the story of God. However, our focus is not on the resurrection of clichés and code words but on engagement in the narrative of God's will for the covenant community, the world, and all creation.

The God of the Scriptures and of the historic Christian faith is actively engaged in his creation, in the life of the human race, and in the life of the church. In other words, God is up to something: God has been at work; God is at work; God will continue to be at work until his work is complete. What we must do is move beyond familiar, often tightly held and deeply loved, clichés and catchphrases and their accompanying symbolic acts. We must imaginatively engage in that "something" that God is up to. We must become active participants in the *God plot*. Taken together, the invitation is clear: we are invited to participate in the God plot as we move from settled clichés to holy imagination.

"Who Done It?"--What's in a Plot?

So if we are to talk about engaging imaginatively in the God plot, we probably should first be clear on what we mean by "plot." The concept of plot probably takes many of us back to our middle school literature classes or perhaps to the plot-line of a good novel or an engaging movie. A plot is simply the sequence of events that make up a story. That sequence most often has a beginning, a middle, and an end that are not disconnected but integrally related. Within a well-defined setting, a dilemma often emerges early on. The driving force or motivating purpose for finding a resolution to the dilemma propels the plot forward. Often, even in the search for a resolution, the dilemma intensifies, but ultimately the plot moves toward resolution either by anticipating an answer or actually discovering the answer to the dilemma.

I have always been fascinated by the consistent, repeated plotline followed by TV murder mysteries such as *Monk* or BBC's *Sherlock*. Each follows the same sequence: setting, dilemma, search for resolution, often an intensification of the dilemma, anticipation of resolution, resolution, and then often a celebration that the resolution had been reached.

A setting is quickly established: sometimes a seaside resort in the middle of summer, sometimes a warm movie theater with snow falling outside, or sometimes a suburban home with busy traffic just outside the door. Then it happens! The dilemma that will remain center stage for the remainder of the show explodes into the setting. Someone drowns in the resort's pool, someone is shot on the back row of the theater, or a car runs headlong into the suburban home!

Immediately, the main character sets out to find the answer to the dilemma—who committed the murder? If the resolution appeared as soon as the murder took place, the drama would proceed no further. The plot continues and intensifies: Find the resolution! Find the guilty party! As soon as we think we have discovered the perpetrator, we are pointed in a different direction—only to hit a dead end. So we seek an alternative resolution. Finally after we have seemed to exhaust every possible answer, we begin to clue in on who it might be. And then the moment arrives: the mystery is solved; the dilemma is settled! In the closing moments, we celebrate that the answer has been found and anticipate what life will look like now that the resolution to the dilemma has taken place.

In a truly great drama, we become fully engaged in the plotline. We become so absorbed in it that we become the detectives ourselves. Our imaginations are on full throttle! We hear the piercing scream of the victim and see the shadow of the perpetrator, we immediately begin the search, and we rule out certain possibilities as we tirelessly work toward resolution. Reaching the aha moment seconds before the detective, we even celebrate that we were a step ahead of the "real detective" all along.

So what in the world does this have to do with us? Way beyond disconnected clichés, isolated catchphrases, or symbolic actions detached from the very story in which they occur, God "is up to something"—a sequence of connected, interrelated events, a plot—the God plot. There is a distinct setting within which God makes an invitation. He calls, and the setting is established! With the setting established through a divine call, an enormous struggle ensues in the lives of those who have been called. The dilemma emerges in the God plot. The struggle, the wrestling match, takes place with the very God who established the setting with a call at the start. No wonder the name *Israel* ("God wrestler") becomes the identifying name for those engaged in the dilemma. With the dilemma established, the search for a resolution begins. Is there any answer? Is there any hope? Even in the search for a resolution, the dilemma intensifies. Hope for an answer far too often ends in dead ends and failures. Yet somehow surely there must be a resolution—a resolution that will be found.

So that is the God plot—or the general idea of it—but what does it mean to us? Everything. To move from the disconnected dots of empty clichés and code words into the interconnected plot of God is to find ourselves imaginatively engaged in not only what God has done in the past but also what God is doing now. Bernhard Anderson has perhaps most imaginatively articulated our role in the study that follows: "Do not suppose that this is the kind of drama one can view from a grandstand seat. We are not to be spectators of something that happened once upon a time. . . . Thus, realizing that the Great Dramatist is apt to lure us from the spectator's balcony and put us into the act, we begin our study."[2]

Here is our invitation: Come out of the balcony of disconnected words, clichés, and symbolic actions. Step onto the stage of the most life-transforming plot that has ever been—the God plot. Watch as the dots connect. Take a step back from the isolated parts, and explore the whole—the entirety—of what God is up to. Become a participant in God's story, a character in the divine drama. In this grand mystery of all time and space, become the detective. Engage in the God plot—with holy imagination.

More than One Way to Tell a Story

How is the story of God told? Throughout Scripture and throughout the history of the Christian faith, the people of God have refused to dilute the story of God down to a single voice, to one solitary perspective. Perhaps this refusal was simply a phenomenon of human culture and language, since different groups have their own ways of voicing and articulating reality. Perhaps the incorporation of different voices in Scripture and in the Christian tradition is a purposeful or even subconscious refusal to package God in a single, recognizable "box"—an idol. Whatever the reason, the story of God is articulated in different voices and from different perspectives.

This phenomenon of diverse voices and perspectives is especially noticeable in the case of the four Gospels. While the Gospels share a common emphasis on the ministry of Jesus Christ, each Gospel is unique, possessing a distinct language and authorship and emerging from a particular community with specific interests and theological convictions about Jesus. Each Gospel articulates the Jesus story, but the perspective from which each tells the story gives us different entry points into the life of Jesus: the suffering and dying King in Mark, the long-expected Jewish Messiah in Matthew, the Savior of all peoples and Friend to the outcast in Luke-Acts, and the preexistent Son of God in the flesh in John. We see the diverse perspectives, and we celebrate them!

However, the Gospels are not the only place with voices that provide different entry points into the story of God. Something very similar occurs in the Old Testament. While many hands contributed to the emergence of the Old Testament, these hands often reflect one of two dominant voices that express distinct ways of thinking and speaking. We can best describe these two voices as the *prophetic* voice and the *priestly* voice. Rather than standing in opposition to each other, these voices are much more like singers who bring their voices—soprano, alto, tenor, and bass—together into a quartet. Each voice makes a significant contribution, but as each voice complements the other, a beautiful harmony emerges. However, like listening to a quartet, it is possible in the study of the Old Testament to lean into one voice and miss the other. At times, our songs, our prayers, our sermons and teachings, even entire religious traditions use the language and thought that emerges from one voice while ignoring the other voice entirely. To hear both voices—the prophetic and the priestly—and then to listen to them sing with and to each other allows us to appreciate the beautiful depth, width, and breadth of the God plot in full harmony.

So before we step onto the stage of the God plot, acquainting ourselves with these two significant voices is essential to our study. For the "Bible study junkie," even a brief overview of these voices will be intriguing and will probably provoke further study on these voices alone. On the other hand, for those who simply want to get on with the God plot itself, a brief overview of these voices may seem like a digression. However, familiarizing ourselves with them will set the stage for a much deeper appreciation and understanding not only of these voices but also of the the way they go about presenting the God plot. Because the formation of these voices is itself a plot, we'll look at it in five *episodes*.

Episode One: The Rise of the Prophetic Voice

Although we will refer to one voice as *prophetic* and to the other as *priestly*, both voices originate in the priesthood of Israel. It is important for us to remember what the primary tasks of the priests were. Certainly priests were responsible for overseeing the worship sites and the sacrifices that occurred at those sites. However, a primary responsibility of the priests that we often overlook was the task of instruction. They had the responsibility for *torah* in the life of the community. While over time we have come to translate the word *torah* as "law," it has a much deeper and wider meaning than simply law. At its core, the term means "instruction." In fact, the verb from which the word *torah* comes (*yarah*) actually means "to teach" or "to instruct." This teaching functions to remind the people of God *both* of their identity through narratives of what God has done *and* of the ethic or lifestyle that emerges out of their identity.

What becomes the *prophetic* voice in the Bible has its origins in one of the twelve sons of Jacob, the sons who serve as the fathers of the twelve tribes of Israel. As the different tribes received their allotted tribal land under the leadership of Joshua, one of those tribes was excepted and did not receive land: the tribe of Levi. Rather than living in its own tribal allotment, the tribe of Levi was to live scattered throughout the various other tribes, serving as priests for the entire people of Israel. According to the biblical narrative, the Levites served as the sole priests of Israel up until the time of King David.

Episode Two: The Emergence of the Priestly Voice

One of David's early significant victories was the conquest of the Canaanite city-state of Jebus or Salem. One of our first introductions to this city is in the journeys of Abraham. In Genesis 14:18, Abraham encounters a king-priest in the city of Salem by the name of Melchizedek. Melchizedek is a priest of El Elyon, God Most High. Because David conquered the city with his own army, the city became his. It truly was "the city of David." Later renamed Jerusalem, the city did not belong to northern tribes or southern tribes. Thus it became the perfect religious and political capital for David's kingdom. Technically it was "neutral territory"; it was like the District of Columbia, which, as the United States capital, does not belong to any particular state. When David brought the ark of the covenant into Jerusalem, he made the city not only the political capital but also the religious capital. As the site that would house the sacred ark of the covenant, Jerusalem would gain the allegiance of all Israelites, both northern and southern. Eventually Solomon's construction of a temple for the ark of the covenant "sealed the deal."

However, David immediately had a problem. As reflected in the early story of Abraham's encounter with Melchizedek, a priesthood already existed in the city. We will refer to this priestly family as the Zadokites. How could David simply remove this family of priests and replace them with the Levites who had been serving as priests for centuries? He didn't. He allowed the Levitical priests and the Zadokite priests to work side by side. Certainly the great tradition of the encounter between the patriarch Abraham and the patriarch of this priestly family, Melchizedek, provided strong rationale for not simply removing this priestly family from Jerusalem worship.

Episode Three: The Plot Thickens

As Solomon came to the throne, a drastic change occurred in the priesthood. Call it political (it seems God's people have always struggled with their own set of political

issues), but the struggle over who would be David's successor to the throne resulted in the removal of the Levitical
priesthood from the Jerusalem temple. It almost sounds like
the plot of a biblical soap opera. On the one hand, the primary Levitical priest, Abiathar, supported Solomon's brother Adonijah, while on the other hand, the primary Zadokite
priest, Zadok, supported Solomon (for a detailed depiction
of the palace intrigue, see the first chapter of 1 Kings). Obviously, once Solomon was established on the throne, the
Zadokite priesthood was rewarded and the Levitical priesthood was demoted. The Levitical priests were removed to
the worship sites outside of Jerusalem, particularly to those
sites that would become the northern kingdom, and with
their movement to these areas eventually went their voice.
Continuing to be identified with the southern kingdom of
Judah, the Zadokite priesthood remained responsible for
the worship that took place in the Jerusalem temple.

Great voices of the Levitical priesthood in the north are
heard in such prophets as Elijah and Elisha as well as the
northern prophet Hosea. Although the prophet Jeremiah
carried out his ministry well after the northern kingdom fell,
his hometown of Anathoth was located in the northern kingdom. His preaching to the southern kingdom clearly reflects
the voice of the northern Levitical priesthood. Reflecting the
thought of the Levitical priests, these individuals articulate
the prophetic voice of the Old Testament. The heartbeat and
concerns of the book of Deuteronomy particularly reflect
many of the northern Levitical convictions about God and
about God's people. In fact, we could very easily call this
northern priestly-prophetic voice the Deuteronomic voice of
the Bible. That voice is embodied in the book of Deuterono-

my and the literary-theological masterpiece that consists of Joshua, Judges, Samuel, and Kings (called by some the Deuteronomistic History because it is a history of Israel written from the perspective of the prophetic-Deuteronomic voice). As we read the books of Deuteronomy, Joshua–2 Kings (with the exception of Ruth), Hosea, and Jeremiah, we soon become aware of their family resemblance to each other; they share common interests and themes and a common language and theological understanding.

Meanwhile, the Zadokite-priestly voice is expressed most particularly in the book of Leviticus. In fact, Leviticus is to the priestly voice what Deuteronomy is to the prophetic voice. These two books are clear expressions of the faith and practices of their respective voices. Likewise, much of the material in Genesis and Exodus demonstrates this priestly voice. Eventually, much later in the history of God's people, a second history was written, a history that reflected the great priestly concerns in the same way that Joshua–Kings reflected the great prophetic concerns. We find this history in 1 and 2 Chronicles and Ezra-Nehemiah. Here David, founder of Israelite worship, and Solomon, builder of the Jerusalem temple, are the twin pillars. The whole story ends in 2 Chronicles with the charge to go up and rebuild the temple in Jerusalem. Although he was called to the prophetic ministry while in exile in Babylon, the prophet Ezekiel also clearly expresses the priestly language and understanding. This is so because he was among the priests in Jerusalem taken into exile. He particularly demonstrates the priestly concerns and language of holy/profane, cleanness/uncleanness, and purity/impurity. As he carries out the prophetic ministry in Babylon, Ezekiel vividly reflects the intertwining of both the prophetic and the priestly voices. We will explore how Ezekiel does this interweaving in later chapters.

Episode Four: The End of the Northern Kingdom of Israel

When the northern kingdom of Israel and its capital at Samaria fell to the Assyrian Empire in 722/721 BC, it is highly likely that at least some of the northern priests, those representing the prophetic voice, migrated down into the still-standing southern kingdom. Once there, they would likely have deposited their instruction (*torah*) of Moses in the Jerusalem temple. It is highly likely that the core of their instruction is found in the book of Deuteronomy. A century after the northern kingdom fell and the migration occurred, the *torah* of Moses was discovered at the time of a temple cleaning. Josiah was king at that time. After the prophetess Huldah affirmed its authenticity, Josiah led the people through a great reform, a revival. Believing that this reform was based on at least the core of the book of Deuteronomy, biblical students will even refer to the reform as the Josianic reform or the Deuteronomic reform. In many ways, Deuteronomy functions as the first "Bible" for the people of God, with its written code becoming the basis of their rediscovered identity and the lifestyle that is to express that identity.

Episode Five: Exile, Postexile, and Beyond . . .

Within forty years after the great reform under Josiah, the southern kingdom fell to the Babylonians. During the half century of the exilic period, the voices attempted to make sense of what occurred. Carried away with the elite and powerful, the Zadokite prophet Ezekiel did this using his priestly language. Staying behind in the vicinity of Jerusalem with the less powerful and the masses and eventually taken down into Egypt, the Levitical prophet Jeremiah did the same using his prophetic language.

After the people returned from exile and the temple was rebuilt, the two voices continued to survive. Obviously, as with all groups, these voices morphed as they faced new challenges. However, we continue to hear and see central convictions expressed. Even as the empire of the Greeks and eventually that of the Romans rose and the people of God were threatened by enculturation, these theological voices evolved and changed. However, the seed planted by the early Zadokite and Levitical priests remained. Certainly by the second century BC, the power structure of the priestly Zadokites, now known as the Sadducees, remained in power in the temple. The prophetic voice that had always stood up against the powers and structures continued to do so. They were determined to remain faithful to Yahweh and to his covenant. Based upon the word *hesed* ("faithful," "loyal"), they became known as the *Hasidim* ("faithful ones"). Eventually emerging out of the *Hasidim* was the group most committed to remaining distinct from the empire and its enculturation while continuing to live within the culture, the Pharisees.

It is indeed fascinating that when Jesus was asked by these two groups what the greatest commandment was, he quoted directly from their early "theological handbooks"—Deuteronomy and Leviticus. In fact, the question seems to be less about what the greatest commandment is than about whose side Jesus was really on.

As we consider the unfolding of the God plot—from setting to call, dilemma to resolution, we will explore the manner in which each voice recounts the story of the covenant God and his covenant people. As observed earlier, individuals and traditions can become unknowingly attached to one of the two dominant voices as that particular voice recalls the plot of God. However, when the two voices are in dialogue with each other, they can enhance our understanding of what God is doing and how he is inviting us to participate in the divine plot.

PART I

The God Plot—Prophetic Style

How did the prophetic voice understand and imaginatively talk about what God was up to? How did this voice tell the God story? In the chapters that follow we will look at the God plot from the prophetic perspective. We will explore how the prophetic voice viewed the setting of the God plot, God's call upon the life of his people, and the people's struggle to faithfully participate with God in his call. We will also discover those things to which the people repeatedly succumbed and fell and examine why they did so. Perhaps most importantly, in the light of the people's consistent struggle and repeated failure to embody the divine call, we will consider the possibility of the God plot ending without resolution. We will search for a hint that the God plot may not end in futility but will actually reach its desired end or purpose (Gk., *telos*) so that the people of God will be able to carry out the divine call in their lives.

one

SETTING
IT'S ALL ABOUT GRACE

GREAT STORIES possess not only great beginnings but also great contexts. They have image-evoking backdrops. If there ever was a great story with the most remarkable of settings, it is certainly the story of God and his people as expressed by the prophetic voice.

Before God ever called his people to be, to do, or to say anything, he acted decisively in their lives. Indeed, divine action consistently preceded divine call. God's initiative came before any human response. Really, this makes sense, doesn't it? How can anyone *respond* if there is nothing to respond to? As the prophetic voice creatively weaves the story of God together, it is insistent that God never invited his people to participate in his story without first opening the entry door into it.

For the people of God, divine grace was not a mere abstract principle to debate. It was not a sentimental concept to incorporate into a prayer, song, or sermon. God's grace was concretely expressed and experienced in real life. Divine action took place in the flesh-and-blood realities of daily existence. The prophetic voice paints an engaging portrait of the gracious entry door opened by God so that his people might actively join him in his divine plot.

The Three Hinges of God's Gracious Activity

The entry door of God's story hangs on three hinges, three pivotal actions carried out by God: divine deliverance, divine provision, and divine covenant. These hinges inform everything else in the God plot. They point to God's character; they form his people's identity; and they undergird the divine call upon the life of the people. They even shape the pattern of their everyday life; as God has acted to deliver, provide, and enter into covenant, so now are his people to act in the lives of their neighbors.

The very core of the people's self-understanding was based on the hinges of God's deliverance, provision, and covenant. Because he was a delivering God, they were a people set free from oppression and captivity. Because he was a providing God, they were a people who had the necessary provisions of life: food, water, and protection from destructive enemies. Because he was a covenant-making God, they were a people in covenant relationship with him and with one another. Just as institutions will often speak of the core values that define their identity and shape their behavior, our ancestors discovered their core values in the narrative of God's deliverance, provision, and covenant. These values defined them, shaped them, and motivated them.

To live within the identity-shaping reality of these three hinges of grace was to live as the people of God. On the other hand, to live outside of the reality of these hinges of grace was to abandon the very identity as a people in covenant with this unique God. To seek deliverance from any other powers, to seek provision from any other sources, to enter into covenant with any other partners in order to secure life was to forsake the identity of being God's people. Two voices clearly associated with this prophetic way of expressing the God plot—Hosea and Jeremiah—would go as far as to call such exchanges of identity as infidelity, adultery, or even prostitution (Hos. 2:2-13; 4:12-19; 5:3-4; Jer. 2:9-37; 3:1-5).

At the very core of the prophetic testimony of God's gracious activity was God's deliverance of his people from captivity. The people of God were well aware that at one time they had been slaves in Egypt, but now they were free! They once had built pyramids for kings they did not know and temples for gods they did not worship, but now they were singing the song of liberation and dancing to the melody of a hope-filled future. The powers that enslaved lost their grip on the oppressed when this God showed up. Iron chariots and mighty horses that terrorized and intimidated were no match for the God who liberates and delivers. No wonder one of the earliest hymns in our Scriptures is the jubilant song of Miriam as she played her tambourine and danced with the other women, singing, "Sing to the LORD, for he has triumphed gloriously; horse and rider he has thrown into the sea" (Exod. 15:21). Their history of bondage had been transformed to a future of hope. Stepping down into the deathly waters of the Red Sea as slaves, they arose from those waters to new life, new freedom, and a new tomorrow.

However, God had not simply freed his people from slavery to let them survive on their own. The God who freed from captivity was also the God who provided in the wilderness—not just once but over and over again. The memories and testimonies of God's people were filled with stories of manna, quail, water, and divine protection.

That first morning of their deliverance from Egyptian captivity, the people stepped out of their tents hungry and thirsty. How would they survive? How would they be nourished in this arid wasteland? As they looked out over the desert, the early morning dew caused something to glisten like diamonds. Looking at this glistening stuff, they exclaimed, *"Mannah? Mannah?"* Or literally, "What is it? What is it?" Lifting up a piece of this odd stuff to their mouths, they tasted it. Discovering the nourishment God had provided them, the answer to their question was, "This is bread from heaven!" The God who had delivered them also provided for them. And the provision continued as they threw their nets over their source of protein for the wilderness journey: lowly migrating quail. The people of God once again witnessed that the God who had delivered them from captivity would also nourish them. In their thirst, they began to murmur as they asked, "How will our parched tongues be quenched?" Suddenly from the rock flowed an oasis of water. Indeed, over and over again, the God who had emancipated them from their captivity demonstrated that he would now provide nourishment for their hunger and drink for their thirst. Indeed, this God provides.

The people's experience of God's grace went beyond a one-time deliverance and one-time provision. Grace overran the banks of the Red Sea and overflowed far beyond the baskets of manna and quail in the wilderness. The God who had graciously delivered at the sea and who had graciously poured out provisions in the wilderness now committed himself to be the delivering and providing God into perpetuity. Graciously initiating a covenant with the people whom he had emancipated and sustained, he announced, "I will be God to you, and you will be people to me" (Exod. 6:7, author's translation). Within this covenant formula was the divine commitment that he would continue to act as the delivering and providing God of this community.

The God who delivered one generation across the Red Sea into the wilderness would deliver the next generation across the Jordan River into the Land of Promise. That same God would deliver a generation from exile centuries later; however, this time he would deliver his people across an arid desert from Babylon to the Promised Land. For one generation, this covenant God is the *Way Maker* across the sea; for another generation, this covenant God is the *Way Maker* across the arid desert. What he does for a later generation may indeed be a new thing, but the new thing remains consistently grounded in the age-old confession that he is the covenant-making God who will consistently deliver and provide regardless of the context within which a given generation finds itself:

> Thus says the LORD, who *makes a way* in the sea, a path in the mighty waters, who brings out chariot and horse, army and warrior; they lie down, they cannot rise, they are extinguished, quenched like a wick: Do not remember the former things, or consider the things of old. I am about to do a new thing; now it springs forth, do you

grace

not perceive it? I will *make a way* in the wilderness and
rivers in the desert. (Isa. 43:16-19, emphasis added)
This God of deliverance and provision is the faithful covenant-making Partner yesterday, today, and tomorrow.

The Tapestry of Giants

Following the gracious acts of God's deliverance, provision, and covenant with his people, Moses delivers in the
book of Deuteronomy an image-filled and image-evoking
sermon to the second generation. Forty years had passed
since that momentous event of Israel's escape from Egypt
and trek across the Red Sea. For forty years, God had faithfully provided food, drink, and protection to his people. In
the midst of these four decades of God's grace and fidelity,
a covenant had been sealed between God and his people.

But very early in the journey, the covenant people struggled with what would become the perennial, nagging problem faced by people in covenant with God. They just seemed
unable to wholeheartedly trust this God who had delivered
them. They just could not fully believe that he really would
continue to provide for them.

Shortly after all the great covenant events surrounding
Mount Sinai, God instructed the people: "You have stayed
long enough at this mountain. Resume your journey. . . .
go in and take possession of the land that I swore to your
ancestors" (Deut. 1:6-7, 8). All seemed hopeful, but then
came the giants! Oh, those giants and the terror, the inse-
curity, and the lack of trust that they always seem to evoke.
In Moses' sermon, his focus shifts to those giants. "Giants"
become the color-filled thread interwoven throughout the

tapestry of the people's interaction with God for the next two chapters of the sermon.

At the start, it was giants that caused an entire generation to fear and to fail. Out of anxious fear, the people of this generation refused to set foot into God's promise for a tomorrow. They concluded that the land with its mighty fortresses and huge warriors was far too big and overpowering. On the one hand, the spies brought back an amazingly optimistic report: "It is a good land that the LORD our God is giving us" (1:25). But the positive report of promise was tempered with the reality that "the people are stronger and taller than we; the cities are large and fortified up to heaven! We actually saw there the offspring of the Anakim!" (v. 28). Anakim are the giants.

The people who were well on their way into the Land of Promise concluded that it was up to them to fight the giants. They became terrified. They grumbled and rebelled. They even accused God himself of despising them. Moses could only make one conclusion. In spite of God's promise to go with his people; to fight for them, as he had done in Egypt; and to carry them like a parent carrying an infant, as he had done in the wilderness, the people would not trust the Lord (vv. 30-32). Their distrustful fear and anxiety would eventually come back on them in full force; not a single member of that generation, with the exception of the two who knew that the battle was ultimately the Lord's, would set foot in the territory of God's promise. Paralyzing fear and a debilitating lack of trust stopped the faith journey short.

Indeed, the story of God for that first generation had originally had so much more to it than death in the wilderness. The God plot was intended to continue on into the land of God's promise; it was not supposed to end in the arid desert. Manna and water-producing rocks only pointed forward to a land that flowed with milk and honey. The delivering, providing, covenant-making God had only begun to carry out his plot in the life of his covenant people.

Divine grace indeed provided the backdrop; divine deliverance, provision, and covenant composed the setting of all that was supposed to follow! The God plot was well on its way for that generation. How tragic! Because of their fear and distrust, the people of that generation would spend the rest of their lives wandering in the wilderness of their doubt. They would die outside of the land of God's promise, and for them the God plot ended with no more than a period or a question mark.

However, the fuller God plot never ends with a period or a question mark. Indeed, the most common punctuation mark in the narrative of God consists of ellipsis points— dot, dot, dot. The God plot would continue through the next generation. Forty years had now passed since the crossing of the sea. As the former generation had died off, a new generation had emerged. It was now time for Moses to prepare the people of the second generation to cross the Jordan and to enter into God's territory of promise that their parents and grandparents had forfeited. In order to prepare them to enter, Moses reminds them of instances when this generation could readily have been terrified at what lay ahead. When King Sihon refused to let the people go through his land, this generation could have thrown its hands up in fear and become paralyzed. However, the Lord was faithful so that "there was no citadel too high for us. The Lord our God gave everything to us" (2:36).

Then there was Og of the land of Bashan (3:1-21)! Once again, a giant with giant resources and giant fortresses appears in the story. It seems that the people of God just couldn't escape running into those giants that threatened to paralyze them with fear. The land of Bashan was renowned for its rich, luxurious natural resources. Its fertile land produced fat, sleek, healthy cattle. The land of Og had fortress cities with extensively high walls, double gates, and strong bars. Numerous outlying villages dotted the landscape. The land of Bashan was "strong," but even more, its ruler, Og, was a giant—a Rephaim (see explanation of all of the terms for giants in 2:20-21). His bed was made of the preferred metal of the day, iron. It was nine cubits long and four cubits wide; that's approximately thirteen feet long by six feet wide. Indeed, it was a strong, mammoth bed for a large, mighty warrior. What does Moses have to say to this generation about the delivering, providing, covenant-making God in the face of such terrorizing, paralyzing giants? "Do not fear him, for I have handed him over to you. . . . So the Lord our God also handed over to us King Og of Bashan" (3:2-3).

The delivering, providing, covenant-making God was faithful in leading his people through the bewildering land of Sihon and Og. The people of the previous generation had thought it was their responsibility to save their own lives and to wage their own war against the threatening giants. Fear-filled paralysis set in and they spent their lives in the wilderness without setting foot into the land of God's promise. Nevertheless, God continued to demonstrate his trustworthiness and his covenant faithfulness over and over again. He faithfully guided his covenant people through the land of giants. Indeed, the people of the generation who thought the battle against the giants was theirs to fight died in the wilderness. However, the generation who looked into the face of fear-evoking giants and dared to declare "You come to me with sword and spear and javelin; but I come to you in the name of the LORD of hosts" (1 Sam. 17:45) saw the giants fall and witnessed the ongoing gracious, delivering, providing, covenant-making acts of God. No wonder Moses concludes the introduction to his prophetic sermon in Deuteronomy with these words: "Your own eyes have seen everything that the LORD your God has done to these two kings; so the LORD will do to all the kingdoms into which you are about to cross. Do not fear them, for it is the LORD your God who fights for you" (Deut. 3:21-22).

So let's think for a moment about divine grace in the matter of giants. To live in the reality of divine grace is to recognize that imminent giants are not ours to fight. The battle is not ours; the battle is the Lord's. On the other hand, to live outside of the reality of divine grace is to believe and ultimately to live out life with the idea that battling the giants is up to us. We naively believe that we must produce the weapons, plan the battle, run into the valley, and slay the giants. To live outside the reality of divine grace is to be consumed with our own survival and to discover and employ every tactic available just to survive.

A Challenge for the Next Generation

Just as Moses prepared a generation to enter into the Land of Promise in his sermon in Deuteronomy, his successor, Joshua, instructed that same generation and their children to settle down and live in the land of God's promise. In so many ways, Joshua's sermon to the people in Joshua 24 is a microcosm of Moses' much more detailed sermon in Deuteronomy. As the people gather in the valley of Shechem, Joshua challenges them to make a decision: choose which god you will worship and devote your lives to. The options are many: the gods of the past, the gods of the popular culture, or the God who delivered, provided, and made covenant with a ragtag group of escapees from Egypt. In an outburst of decisiveness, Joshua then exclaims, "As for me and my clan, we will serve the LORD" (v. 15, author's paraphrase).

It is so fascinating, however, that before Joshua ever challenges the people to choose some god to whom they will give their devotion, he lays out a thorough, detailed overview of all that the Lord had already done in their lives. The rehearsal of divine actions is filled with God's faithful, continuous deliverance and provision:

> I took your father Abraham. . . . I gave him Isaac. . . . to Isaac I gave Jacob and Esau. . . . I gave Esau the hill country. . . . I sent Moses and Aaron. . . . I plagued Egypt. . . . I brought [you] out of Egypt. . . . [I] put darkness between you and the Egyptians. . . . your eyes saw what I did to Egypt. . . . I brought you to the land. . . . I handed them over to you. . . . I would not listen to Balaam. . . . I rescued you out of his hand. (Vv. 3-10)

Just before Joshua challenges the people of God to serve the Lord God with undivided allegiance or at least to choose some god to worship, he concludes his detailed review with these image-evoking words: "It was not by your sword or by your bow. I gave you a land on which you had not labored, and towns that you had not built, and you live in them; you eat the fruit of vineyards and oliveyards that you did not plant" (vv. 12-13).

Do you see it? Can you hear it? Before Moses and Joshua ever call the people of God to do, to be, or to say anything, they are adamant about the context of the story of God. They are unrelentingly persistent on the setting of the God plot. The core identity of the people of God is not found in their own productivity, achievement, or accomplishment. They did not build their own bridges across the Red Sea or the Jordan River; they did not produce their own manna; they did not slay their giants by the strength of their warriors; they did not plant their own vineyards and dig out their own wells. No, indeed, they are solely and uniquely the recipients of gracious divine deliverance, provision, and covenant. At the very core of their identity, the people of God are the blessed, the graced, and the gifted children of God.

Before a call or a challenge ever goes out to God's people, they *already* have the identity of being recipients of divine grace. They are recipients of divine love as no other—that is, holy love. They are recipients of incomparable divine mercy. The Lord has delivered them. The Lord has provided for them. The Lord has entered into covenant with them. He will continue to be their God, and they will be his people—a people of deliverance and a people of provision.

The Kingdom Prayer: Give Us Daily Bread....Deliver Us from Evil

Across space and time, the people in covenant with this delivering and providing God have realized that they are defined by an alternative reality. They belong to a different kingdom with a radically unique (holy) politic for deliverance and a radically unique (holy) economy for provision. God is the Source of both, not themselves!

When facing the onslaught of giant-sized enemies that seek to devour them and spit them out, they seem to understand, or at least deep down they know they should understand, that they themselves are not the source of their deliverance. This unique covenant-making God is the Source. When facing even their own death and potential demise, they confess, or at least they know they should confess, that their own manipulative devices, controlling schemes, and power-playing games will never deliver them. This covenant-making God alone is their Deliverer. It is no wonder then that they would pray, "Lead us not to the time of trial, but *you deliver* us from evil!" (see Matt. 6:13).

When facing hunger and thirst, these people in covenant with this graciously providing God seem to understand, or at least they know they should understand, that they themselves cannot engage in the "hunger games" to guarantee their lone survival. This unique covenant-making God alone provides manna to the hungry and water to the thirsty. When dwindling bank accounts and dying congregations seem to threaten their very survival and existence, these people in covenant with this graciously providing God seem to understand, or at least they know they should understand, that they could never manipulate fertility or magically coerce resurrection. This unique covenant-making God alone gives life to the lifeless and breath to the dying. It is no wonder then that they would pray, "Give us today our daily bread" (v. 11, NIV).

Embrel.com
without insurance
safetynet
elisbil

And what would they call a politic in which God delivers from all that destroys and an economy in which God provides the daily bread? "Your kingdom come: your will be done on earth as it is in heaven" (see v. 10). These people in covenant with the unique (holy) God who delivers and provides seem to know, or at least they know they should know, that there is a radical alternative to self-sustaining survival and to self-fought deliverance. They have even referred to that alternative as the reign of God on earth, the kingdom of God. To say it another way: they dare to believe and hope that this unique (holy) delivering, providing, covenanting God engages in the real-life world of every man and every woman in every land each and every day. And so they pray, "May your heavenly will come right down to earth: may *you* provide today's *manna,* and may *you* deliver from all that would destroy."

Grace: Great to Experience Now but All Too Easy to Forget Tomorrow

Why would recitals of God's gracious deliverance and provision appear throughout Scripture? There just seems to be the recognition that we human beings are all too easily prone to amnesia. As we fail to remember the delivering, providing, and covenanting character of this unique (holy) God, we quickly forget what he has done. In our amnesia of who God is and what God has done, we then forget who we are (delivered, provided, covenanted people). And in our forgetting who we are, we turn our attention to and make covenant with everything and everyone else that promises to deliver and to provide.

The attention of our biblical ancestors very quickly would turn to the options of other gods offered by the dominant, popular culture in which they lived. Failure to remember and failure to tell the next generation of this unique covenant God's faithfulness are always linked to the warning not to turn to the gods of pop culture. It makes sense that in Moses' sermon (Deuteronomy) to the second generation that did not have the privilege of being eyewitnesses to God's defining moments of deliverance and provision, Moses makes repeated calls to remember and to not forget.

In Deuteronomy 6:12, Moses challenges the people to be extremely careful (literally, *to guard* or *to protectively watch*) not to "forget the LORD, who brought [them] out of the land of Egypt." How easy it would be to look at the majestic, large cities that they did not build, the houses filled with all types of goods that they had nothing to do with achieving, the smooth-stoned wells that they did not manufacture, and the fertile vineyards and olive groves that they did not even plant and to conclude that all of this was the achievement of their own hard work and efforts.

Later, in Deuteronomy 8:11-20, in the light of the people's full bellies, well-constructed houses, fertile herds, and abundant wealth, Moses warns them not to exalt themselves and *forget* the Lord, who had accomplished all of this for them. And how would they forget the Lord? Moses was certainly not concerned that they would miss the answers in a round of Bible trivia. His concern was that they would end up concluding, "My power and the might of my own hand have gotten me this wealth" (v. 17).

Integral to the prophetic call to *remember and not forget* the Lord is the challenge to rehearse over and over all that

God had done. The only way the next generation can ever know the faithfulness and the gracious actions of this unique God is for the preceding generations to pass the story on. One generation must give witness to what preceding generations have seen and heard God do. This witness includes not only verbal testimonies about God's faithfulness but also the creation of signs and symbols that will cause future generations to ask the most significant question in learning: "What is that?" Once curiosity is invoked, the "testifying generation" will have the most opportune setting in which to share the *good news* of God's fidelity. However, when the "testifying generation" remains silent or simply settles for empty clichés, amnesia overpowers that generation and ignorance overpowers the subsequent generation.

In the next chapter, we will explore in detail the pivotal prophetic call upon the lives of God's people expressed in the *Shema,* or the call to love the Lord with all the heart, soul, and strength (see 6:4-5). Immediately after his call for undivided loyalty to the Lord, Moses exhorts the people to give their attention to rehearsing the story of God "when you are at home and when you are away, when you lie down and when you rise" (v. 7). When future generations ask why the people live life as they do, the "testifying generation" is to answer, "We were Pharaoh's slaves in Egypt, but the LORD brought us out of Egypt with a mighty hand" (v. 21).

The context of God's gracious activity through his deliverance of, provision for, and covenant with his people goes hand in hand with the repeated concern to remember and not forget and to tell the next generation. Amnesia and ignorance can all too easily consume and destroy the foundational identity of grace. This concern for remembrance is a vibrant thread interwoven throughout the ongoing story of God's people. Immediately after the people crossed the Jordan River into the Land of Promise, Joshua selected a man from each of the twelve tribes. He instructed each of them to take a stone out of the river and to pile the stones at Gilgal. This pile of stones would function as a *sign* among the people so that when future generations ask "What do those stones mean to you?" they would proceed to tell them how the waters of the river were "cut off in front of the ark of the covenant of the LORD" (Josh. 4:6-7).

Once the various tribes settled into their allotments of land, they gathered in the village of Shechem to renew their covenant with the Lord (chaps. 23–24). As we mentioned earlier, before Joshua ever calls upon them to choose a deity to worship (24:14-15), he goes into extensive detail reminding the second generation of all that the Lord has done in their lives, concluding with the declarations, "It was not by your sword or by your bow" and "I gave you a land on which you had not labored, and towns that you had not built" (vv. 12-13).

Once settled in the land, a statement very early in the book of Judges articulates the fruit of a generation growing up unaware of its identity as the graced people of this covenant God: "Another generation grew up after them, who did not *know* the LORD or the work that he had done for Israel" (Judg. 2:10, emphasis added). The next two verses depict what becomes the perennial dilemma of the people of God: "Then the Israelites did what was evil in the sight of the LORD and worshiped the Baals; and they abandoned the LORD, the God of their ancestors, who had brought them out of the land of Egypt; they followed other gods, from among the gods of the peoples who were all around them" (vv. 11-12).

It would be very tempting to point a finger at the people of this generation who did evil, abandoned the Lord, and followed the gods of pop culture. However, we just can't put the blame on them! How could they remain faithful to a God whom they did not even know? Why would they worship a God of whom they had heard nothing or, perhaps at best, only sentimental clichés? If the only god of whom they were aware was the god made popular by the dominant culture or the empire itself, it only makes sense that they would turn to the god with whom they were familiar. Even if they would continue to use the familiar, sentimental language of a god by the name of Yahweh, they would simply understand and worship that deity as another god of the pop culture. It just doesn't make sense for a subsequent generation to give allegiance and wholehearted loyalty to a god it doesn't even know!

In spite of the repeated reality of amnesia and ignorance, the insistent concern to remember and not forget and to tell continues to reappear throughout the thread of the plot of God and his people. After a victorious battle, Samuel set up the *Ebenezer* ("stone of assistance") so it could give testimony to both the present and future generations: "Up to this point the LORD has [assisted] us" (1 Sam. 7:12, NLT). In his farewell address (12:6-18), Samuel provides a recitation of "all the saving deeds of the LORD that he performed" (v. 7). Describing the people's forgetfulness of all that the Lord had done after Moses and Aaron had led them out of Egypt, Samuel recalls the activity of God through such judges as Jephthah and Samson.

In the next generation, in spite of all of the mighty trials that David had experienced from the hands of his enemies both outside and inside his family, the king looks back on his life and celebrates the Lord's faithfulness in a remarkable expression of gratitude. Lifting up his voice in melodic poetry, he summarizes his journey with the Lord in these words: "The LORD is my rock, my fortress, and my deliverer, my God, my rock, in whom I take refuge" (2 Sam. 22:2-3). After an extensive, lengthy recounting of all that the Lord had done in his life, David then concludes, "The LORD lives! Blessed be my rock, and exalted be my God, the rock of my salvation. . . . He is a tower of salvation for his king, and shows steadfast love to his anointed" (vv. 47, 51). What a testimony to future generations of this uniquely gracious, delivering, providing, and covenanting God!

Several centuries later, the classically prophetic voice of the eighth century, Hosea, grieves over the reality that there is "no knowledge of God in the land" (Hos. 4:1). The prophet directly ties the lack of knowledge of God to the lack of fidelity as well as the pervasiveness of violence, dishonesty, stealing, and adultery throughout the land (vv. 1-2). He bemoans that the people in covenant with the delivering and providing God are destroyed because of their "lack of knowledge" (v. 6). According to the prophet Hosea, "Israel has forgotten his Maker" (8:14). As Hosea provides the covenant community with a prayer of repentance, he paints a vivid picture of the deep need for the people to remember their covenant God: "Let us know, let us press on to know the LORD" (6:3).

Finally, in the next century, the other classically prophetic voice of Jeremiah grieves in a manner very similar to Hosea: "My people are foolish, they do not know me; they are stupid children, they have no understanding" (Jer. 4:22). Poignantly asking, "Can a girl forget her ornaments, or a bride her attire?" he concludes, "My people have forgotten me" (2:32).

Grace...Forgotten!

What a remarkable identity: a graced and blessed people through divine deliverance, divine provision, and divine covenant. What a unique (holy) God, gracious and blessing, Deliverer, Provider, Covenant Partner. But of what value is this identity when it is not remembered? Of what significance is the gracious activity of divine deliverance, provision, and covenant when it fails to be confessed to subsequent generations? When diluted to a forgotten cliché, "amazing grace" has a nice ring to it, but its identity-shaping, ethos-forming capacity in the life of God's people is diluted to sheer sentimentality.

two

CALL
UNDIVIDEDLY WHOLE

SO HOW are the people of God to respond to this divine grace? How are they to embody their identity as graced, blessed, and gifted people, rescued from slavery and nourished in the wilderness? How do they live out in a practical, daily manner the reality that they are covenant partners with a God who has promised that he would be their God? To find the prophetic answers to these perplexing questions and others like them, we must begin by taking a look at the Shema.

First found in Deuteronomy 6:4-5 and later repeated by Jesus in the Gospels (Matt. 22:34-40; Mark 12:28-34; Luke 10:25-28), the name *Shema* arises from the opening word of the call that God places upon the lives of his people: *"Hear [shema'], O Israel: The Lord is our God, the Lord alone. You shall love the Lord your God with all your heart, with all your soul, and with all your [strength]"* (Deut. 6:4-5, emphasis added).

While the words of the Shema seem to make sense at first sight, each word is loaded with tremendous meaning that goes beyond a surface reading. So what does it mean to *hear*? What is a *god*? What is the significance of *alone*? What is *love*? What are the *heart,* the *soul,* and the *strength*? Each of these concepts is central to the covenant people's response to God's gracious activity. Each word invites us to go much deeper into its meaning and significance for the lives of our ancestors as well as for our own.

What Does It Really Mean to Hear?

The opening word, *shema',* carries with it the double meaning of "to hear" and "to obey." The call to hear the word of the Lord is simultaneously the call to obey the word of the Lord. For our ancestors, to authentically hear (*shema'*) is to embody or to obey (*shema'*) that which was heard. In like manner, to faithfully obey (*shema'*) the word of the Lord is to have clearly heard (*shema'*) the Lord speak. While the New Testament book of James makes the important distinction between people who simply hear the word and those who both hear the word and do it (1:22), the very nature of the Shema calls upon the covenant people to faithfully live out (i.e., obey) the identity that has been made known to them (i.e., what they have heard). They are not to divide their lives into a supernatural component and a commonplace component. For people in covenant with God, God has invaded the everyday of life. For the Shema, the line that we can all too easily draw between the spiritual and the secular just does not exist. The covenant people faithfully embody in the day-to-day affairs of their lives (no matter how mundane those affairs may be) what they have heard and seen from God.

Israel--a Covenant People; the Lord--a Covenant God

Rather than the call of the Shema being addressed to an undefined, anonymous group of people, it directly addresses the people whom the Lord has delivered and nourished and with whom he has made covenant. The addressees of the Shema are already the covenant people of God. In Deuteronomy 6:4-5, the covenant people are the ancient Israelites who have been delivered from Egyptian captivity. In the Gospels, the covenant people are the followers of Jesus Christ, the church.

Before the Shema ever calls the covenant people to respond, it reminds them of the nature and character of their covenant God. This is not just any generic deity. If it were, the text would use a more generic term, such as *'elohim* (a god or a deity). The statement is not simply *"God* is our god" but rather it is *"the LORD* [*Yahweh*] is our god" (emphasis added). This covenant God is a unique (holy) God with a unique name. This is the God who revealed himself to Moses at the burning bush as Yahweh (Exod. 3:13-16). This is the same God of whom Miriam sings as the mighty deliverer of the Israelites: "Sing to *the LORD* [*Yahweh*], for he has triumphed gloriously" (15:21, emphasis added).

So...What's a god/God?

Yahweh is our *God*. The concept of "a god" makes complete sense, right? Maybe, but maybe not! Before we go any further in our examination of the Shema, it really is significant for us to consider perhaps the most misunderstood word in all of Scripture. We use the word in an almost thoughtless way; it just seems to make sense. But what is a *god*? We can all too easily dilute the meaning of the idea of a god down to simply "important things" or the "most important thing" in life.

A god is undoubtedly an extremely important person or thing, even the most important person or thing in our lives. Certainly a god is the object of worship and adoration. Because we especially define a god as an "important" or the "most important" thing, we find ourselves referring to our careers, houses, and bank accounts as gods. If it is at the top of our list of important things, we call it a god. Somewhere we got the notion that a god is our highest priority. As a result of that notion, we spend all of life rearranging our competing priorities, trying to keep God at the number one position.

However, even in the midst of our juggle to keep the Lord at the top of our list of important things, something or someone else seems to be shaping our priority list. Even while the Lord remains number one on our list, something other than the Lord seems to be informing what is on the list. In reality, whatever is shaping the list is god, not what is number one on the list. A god defines reality, value, and meaning for us. A god is what even tells us that some particular deity may be important enough to put on the list or at the top of the list. That god that shapes reality for us and even determines what makes it on the list varies from person to person and from society to society. It may include such things as individualism, consumerism, productivity, self-security, survival, or even pleasure.

When our biblical ancestors talked about a god, whether that god be Yahweh or any other god, such as the Canaanite Baal, the Babylonian Marduk, or the Moabite Chemosh, they were referring to far more than simply the most important thing in their lives. They knew very well that ultimately a god gave definition to life, since it provided the basis on which all of life was to be understood. It was as if a god were the lens through which all of life was to be viewed, bringing clear focus to certain aspects of life and blurring others. As a god was ultimately the basis or foundation of all reality, the character and the nature of a god would determine the character and the nature of all that existed.

From this understanding of a god, houses and clothing, education and careers, and relationships and bank accounts do not suddenly become "gods" just because they are important in our lives. Something, someone, or some system larger than all of these determines for us that these other things are of value. Whatever it is that is making that determination is the "god." Everything else is simply an expression of the "god" that has determined its value and significance.

The first prohibition in the Ten Commandments, "You shall have no other gods before me" (Exod. 20:3), is by no means a license to make a list of important things as long as the Lord is the most important thing. Actually, the first commandment prohibits bringing any other gods ("definers of reality") into the presence of the Lord. The God who delivers, provides, and makes covenant—that God *alone* with no rivals whatsoever—is to define all that is real. That gracious, covenant-making God is to be the sole lens through which *all* of life is to be viewed. Through the lens of this unique and peculiar delivering, nourishing God, everything else comes into focus or goes out of focus. Thus the first commandment insists that the Lord is no mere "first" on a list of valuable things; the Lord is the One who determines the list itself.

So just who is this Yahweh, this Lord, *our* God? Just as the possessive pronoun "our" indicates, he is uniquely the God who has entered into covenant with a peculiar group of people. In the light of that covenant, those people will resolutely confess him as *our* God. But what does his name tell us about this covenant-making God who defines all reality? What does his name reveal about his character? In explaining his divine name, Yahweh declares to Moses, "I will be whoever I will be" (see 3:14). He then proceeds to make very clear, "You go to Pharaoh, and *I will be* with you. You go to the people, and *I will be* with you. You come back to this mountain, and *I will be* with you." This unique God is not the Zeus of Mount Olympus, who waits for his worshippers to come to where he is in order to worship him. He is the God who accompanies his people on their journey. He is the God whose very character is gracious presence. There is nowhere that his people will go but that he will not go with them. Yet at the very same time, his name/character refuses to allow his covenant people to encapsulate him in a formula, to capture him in a box, or to trap him in an idol. He indeed will be with his people, but he himself will determine *how* he will be with them. He is sovereign presence, transcendent immanence.

The lens through which the people of God were to interpret and embody life was the same self-giving commitment that they had witnessed in this One who revealed his name as Yahweh. In him they saw self-emptying commitment go far beyond a sentimental feeling. They witnessed divine commitment vividly expressed through the concrete actions of deliverance, provision, and covenant making. No greater word articulates this self-emptying commitment and devotion to another than "love." No wonder in his Deuteronomic sermon to the wilderness generation, Moses would say, "It was not because you were more numerous than any other people that the LORD set his heart on you and chose you. . . . It was because the LORD loved you and kept the oath that he swore to your ancestors, that the LORD has brought you out with a mighty hand, and redeemed you from the house of slavery" (Deut. 7:7-8).

The opening statement of the Shema is adamant about what gives definition and shape to all of life: "Yahweh is our God." This God who graciously delivers, provides, and makes covenant is the lens through which the people in covenant with him will see and interpret life. If the reality of self-emptying commitment to "the other" as defined in, by, and through Yahweh gives definition and focus to life, the people in covenant with him will likewise envision and embody life through similar self-emptying commitment to their covenant God and to their neighbor.

Our God Alone or Our God Is One?

The statement by which Moses describes Yahweh in the Shema has been a matter of debate for centuries. Many good study Bibles will often provide a translation in the text itself but then will also provide an alternative translation in a footnote. Actually both translations legitimately reflect central convictions concerning God and his covenant people. One translation articulates a conviction concerning the character of the Lord God himself: "The LORD our God, the LORD is one" (Deut. 6:4, NIV). The other translation articulates a conviction concerning the character or nature of the covenant people's worship: "The LORD is our God, the LORD *alone*" (NRSV, emphasis added).

The translation that speaks of the Lord as one insists on the undivided character of God. This understanding of the "oneness" of God stands in sharp contrast to the popular fertility religions that the Israelites confronted daily. We often refer to this pop religion of the Canaanites as baalism. While we will address several other key ideas and practices of baalism below, a particular understanding of baalism is especially significant in the light of the Shema. Baal was the proper name for a single deity in the ancient Near Eastern pantheon of gods, especially the name of the Syrians' storm god. However, this god would have diverse manifestations at various local worship sites. Because the word *baal* literally means "master" or "lord," each worship site had its own responsible lord or *baal*. For example, references are made to Baal of Gad (Josh. 11:17; 12:7), Baal of Hazor (2 Sam. 13:23), Baal of Hermon (Judg. 3:3), Baal of Peor (Hos. 9:10), and Baal of Tamar (Judg. 20:33). With each locale having its Baal manifestation, there was indeed a *plurality* of the one divine personality.

In contrast to the multiplicity of *baals* worshipped throughout the land, the Shema insists that Yahweh is not a multiplicity. He is one; he is undivided. In contrast to the Baal worshipper who would journey to a local shrine in order to worship at a site of the local divine lord/master (*baal*), worshippers of Yahweh understood that he actually journeyed with them. Clearly, what often became a trap was this popular mind-set in which the worshipper of Yahweh would journey to a site in order to worship, whether that site be Bethel, Gilgal, or even Jerusalem itself. However, the very character of Yahweh insisted that he would not be divided into a Yahweh of Bethel, a Yahweh of Gilgal, or a Yahweh of Jerusalem. He is one, undivided Yahweh.

The unique (holy) God who delivered and provided for his covenant people refused to be locked into a particular shrine in the same way that he refused to be locked into a humanly carved idol. While he may have made himself known at various sites in diverse ways, ultimately this one, undivided Yahweh refused to remain located at one shrine. He was a deity on the move with his people. The essence of the divine name itself reveals this unique (holy) aspect of God's character: "I will be whoever I will be" (see Exod. 3:14). Indeed, his very character was to be present with his people; however, he would never permit his people to determine when, where, or how he was with them.

On the one hand, while the Shema insists on the undivided nature of Yahweh, it likewise insists on the undivided nature of the people or at least the undivided nature of their worship. As the alternative translation reads "The LORD is our God, the LORD alone" (Deut. 6:4, NRSV), the Shema calls upon the covenant people to establish absolutely no rivals to Yahweh. He *alone* is their God. Just as the first translation assumes the popular religious understandings and practices of the day, so, too, does this translation. In our ancestors' world, atheism, or the belief in no god, was practically a nonissue. The psalmist would conclude that the person who says there is no god is simply a fool (Ps. 14:1). In the ancient world, everybody essentially believed in gods. The question was just how many gods a person might believe in, and of those gods, to which ones a community should devote its worship.

This statement in the Shema is not a philosophical assertion that only one god exists (i.e., monotheism, or the belief in one god and one god alone). Rather, this statement asserts that for people in covenant with Yahweh, he is the only god they are to worship (i.e., monolatry, or the worship of only one god). Listen to the words once again: "Hear, O Israel, Yahweh is *our God*, Yahweh *alone*." The very character of this covenant people is that their devotion, trust, and worship were to be directed to one god and to one god alone. The concern was not that they believe in some god but that they devote their lives to a unique and specific god—the God who had graciously delivered them, provided for them, and entered into covenant with them—the Lord God.

While we may prefer one translation of the opening line of the Shema over the other, both translations make extremely significant assertions that express deeply held convictions of the people of God. They both shape the understanding of character. One shapes the understanding of God's character; the other shapes the understanding of the covenant community's character. Oneness, completeness, and undividedness are essential in both. More than a locally worshipped manifestation of a deity, the Lord God is undivided; he is one. Likewise, the covenant community is to be devoted in their worship to *one* God and *one* God *alone*. Indeed, just as the Lord is undivided in his character, so, too, are his people to be undivided in their devotement to him. How then are the people in covenant with this God who is one (undivided) and who is the *sole* God of their worship to respond to his gracious activity of deliverance, provision, and covenant? "Love the LORD your God with all your heart, and with all your soul, and with all your [strength]" (Deut. 6:5).

What's Love?

"Love" may be the most overused word in our vocabulary. On the one hand, we *love* chocolate cake. On the other hand, we *love* to golf or to travel. At the same time, we *love* our family and our friends. And then we gather for worship and sing *love* songs to God as we celebrate the *love* God has for the world. Then we go as far as to say that the very identity of God *is* love. No wonder the people in covenant with God can become quickly confused over what it really means to *love* God.

From time to time, the songs we sing, the testimonies we give, or the prayers we pray seem to reveal that our love for God is comparable to our love for something that gives us personal satisfaction. It satisfies our taste buds; it appeals to our interests; it soothes our appetite. Yet the call to love this covenant God goes far beyond the category of love for chocolate cake, travel, or golf. This call to love God does not emerge from fulfilled taste buds, desires, or self-interests.

At other times, we tend to talk about our love for God with deep fondness or affection. Maybe we even think about it as friendship: God as my BFF! Because we have such deep affection for spouses, children, parents, and friends and speak of our love for them to express that emotionally charged feeling of fondness and warmth, we translate our love toward God in a similar way. However, the call to love the Lord extends even beyond the emotion or affection of highest regard, appreciation, or deep fondness for God.

We are making no judgment against appreciation for what personally satisfies or for affection toward friends and family; however, the essence of the call to "love the LORD your God" goes deeper than appreciation, wider than satisfaction, and broader than affection. This call is rooted within the context of an established relationship between two parties; the call to love God is rooted in covenant. While in the Shema, the call to love occurs within the relationship between God and his people, it could also occur within the relationship between a husband and a wife, between a parent and a child, between an employee and an employer, or between two friends. Within the context of covenant, love is ultimately fidelity. *To love* is to be faithful and trustworthy within an established relationship. *To love* is to maintain consistency within the commitment that has been made between two parties. *To love* is to continue the "I do" of covenant long after the "I do" has been said. For God to love us is for God to be consistently faithful, loyal, and trustworthy in his relationship with us. For us to love God is the same: we are to be faithful, loyal, and trustworthy to the God with whom we share covenant. In the same way, for us to love our spouses, our children, our parents, and our neighbors is a matter of faithfulness and trustworthiness.

The Shema's call *to love* is not the generic emotion of good feelings, the desire for personal satisfaction brought on by another person or thing, or the strong affection or fondness for someone else. Love is commitment. Love is loyalty. Love is fidelity. To say to God or to another person "I love you" communicates loyalty and commitment to the one with whom we have made covenant.

Heart, Soul, Strength

The Shema, however, does not simply stop with the call to love God. It elaborates: "Love the LORD your God with . . . heart . . . soul . . . [strength]" (Deut. 6:5). These terms all seem to make sense, don't they? Three very neat divisions of our lives: our emotions (heart), our spirituality (soul), and our physical bodies (strength). Right? Well, not really! In fact, our biblical ancestors had no concept of dividing us humans into three neatly separated parts. If anything, our biblical ancestors passed a faith to us that understands human beings as *whole* people rather than as people *separated* into distinct parts. The call of the Shema to love God with the heart, soul, and strength is not a call for a tripartite human being but for a whole human being to be undividedly loyal.

Heart? When our ancestors wanted to refer to the source of their emotions, they would actually refer to the kidneys rather than the heart. This actually seems to make more sense. It often seems that when our emotions are running wild, our kidneys can go into overdrive! The heart, or the biblical term *leb*, actually represented the source of human decisions. The concept of the *leb* comes much closer to our understanding of the will or the mind. It incorporates all we understand that goes into the decision-making processes—emotional/affective, intellectual/rational, psychological/sociological, and physiological factors. To love the Lord with all of our heart (*leb*) is to love him with the entirety of our will, our mind, the centerpiece of our daily decision-making processes.

Soul? So what about the soul or what the Bible calls our *nephesh*? For centuries now, when Christians see the word "soul," they tend to think the way the Greeks at the time of

Jesus thought. The Greek understanding was that there was an eternal, spiritual aspect to human beings that was caged in our material bodies, which were deemed as evil. Since this Greek way of thinking believed that anything material was evil, they concluded that salvation was ultimately the escape of this eternal soul from the body. When the body died, the soul could then fly away to its eternal existence. How much more could God show us the fallibility of thinking that material bodies were evil than to wrap himself up in flesh and blood and live among us as a human being in a body? Even more, when his body died, he did not escape from his body and fly away into some kind of spiritual, soul-like existence. His body rose from the dead, and according to Paul, based on the bodily resurrection of Jesus, we, too, will have a bodily resurrection (1 Cor. 15; 1 Thess. 4:13-18).

So if our biblical ancestors did not understand the *nephesh* (soul) to be simply an invisible, spiritual aspect of our inner being, what is it? Perhaps one of the best ways to locate the *nephesh* is to put a couple of your fingers up to the side of your neck just below your ear. Do you feel something? "Sure," you say. "I feel my pulse; my pulse that tells me I am alive." We call that beat a pulse; our ancestors understood that the beat was an indication of *nephesh*: life, life energy, life force. When a knife cuts through that part of the neck, we would say one dies because the jugular vein was cut. Our ancestors understood that the very *nephesh*, the life or life force, of a living being had been destroyed. When biblical stories depict a person who seeks to kill another person, they frequently will describe the murderer as seeking the *nephesh* (the life or soul) of that person. For example, Saul attempts to take David's *nephesh* in 1 Samuel

23:15, and Absalom attempts to take David's *nephesh* in 2 Samuel 16:11. No wonder, when someone is thirsty to the point of death, he or she could speak of his or her *nephesh* as longing for water or his or her *nephesh* (sometimes even translated in our Bibles as "throat" or "neck") as being dry (see Pss. 42:1-2; 63:1, 5). To love the Lord with all of our *soul* is to love the Lord with the entirety of our *lives*, our very life energy or being!

Strength? For the longest time, I loved the third part of the call in the Shema because it gave me my biblical motivation for taking care of my body. I had always read that word "strength" as that part of me that was physical. Thus I am to love the Lord in the way I take care of my body, the way I eat, sleep, and exercise. I especially appreciated the sign that hung over the workout machines in my local Christian gym: "Love the LORD . . . with all your strength." The sign gave me my spiritual motivation to lift an extra ten pounds! Clearly, there are more than enough good motivations both within the Bible and outside of it for the proper care of our physical bodies. However, all of my Shema-oriented motivations for physical exercise came crashing down when I finally discovered that the word translated as "strength" or "might" is actually *me'od*, which literally means "everything." It is as if the writer pauses for a moment after calling upon the people to love the Lord with all of their heart (will or mind) and with all of their soul (life or vitality) and thinks, "What's been left out?" Then after reflecting on anything else that might have been ignored, it is as if the writer takes a deep breath, shrugs his shoulders, and simply says "and all your everything." To love the Lord with all of our *strength* is to love the Lord with *everything*.

Focusing on the Most Significant--
Most Repeated--Word

When we hear God's call to us in the Shema, we appropriately tend to focus on the verb "love" and then to turn our secondary focus on the sources of our love: *heart, soul, strength*. However, in our attention to these words, we all too easily overlook what is the primary and ultimate concern of the prophetic call to the people who have tasted divine deliverance, provision, and covenant. This ultimate concern will become the heartbeat of the repeated, ongoing dilemma for the people of God according to the prophetic voice. The concern appears in the word that occurs three times in the Shema: *all* your heart, *all* your soul, *all* your strength. The call to the people of God is for them to respond to God's gracious actions toward them not simply by loving God but by loving him completely, entirely, undividedly. The predicament that the people of God will have over and over again in the story of Israel as told in Joshua through 2 Kings is not their absence of love for the Lord but their inability to love him alone. Time after time they struggle with divided loyalty, compromised commitment, fragmented faithfulness.

In reality, it would have been extremely difficult for the covenant people to have ever completely abandoned Yahweh. To do so would be the demise of their identity. They knew that he was the God who brought them into existence as a people. Thus he legitimated their very presence among the nations. He truly was their "reason for being." They would never attempt to rewrite their story and attribute their deliverance from Egypt to another god. They would never consider crediting nourishment in the wilderness to some other divine power. It would be absurd for any people of a subsequent generation to become "historical revisionists" and ascribe to another god the covenant that made them a people. At a bare minimum, the Lord would always remain the god of their history and tradition. In this sense, they were "stuck" with Yahweh.

With the complete abandonment of the Lord being ruled out, the perennial struggle of the people was to remain faithful to this God who had delivered them, provided for them, and entered into covenant with them. As situations changed and new challenges emerged, could they truly trust this God who had acted in their past? When new systems that promised life, fertility, abundance, and hope were presented to them, would they trust this God of the previous generation's Egypt and yesterday's wilderness or would they trust the new systems that seemed to promise something "bigger and better," "new and improved"?

Thus the heartbeat of the call upon the covenant people was not simply to be devoted to the Lord but to be devoted to him with total, undivided love. The call was to love this delivering and providing God completely—without rival or competition in loyalties. The call was to "all-ness."

The Call: The Thread That Holds the Plot Together

This divine call to undivided love, to unadulterated fidelity, does not stay tucked away in the Shema. In the dance between the Lord and his people, it is the interwoven thread that holds the God plot together. In an almost haunting way, it reappears in all of its vibrancy just when it seems to have faded away and become lost in the shadows of the past. Although the shades and textures of the language may change, the call to unadulterated fidelity remains consistent throughout the plot of a unique (holy) God who has graciously entered into covenant with a peculiar group of people.

This call to undivided love or devotement is expressed in an abundance of words such as "whole" (*shalom*), "complete" or "perfect" (*tamim*), and "clean" (*tahor*). It occurs in speeches and prayers of leaders and in sermons of prophets. It is articulated through the mouths of great biblical personalities such as Samuel, David, Solomon, and Elijah. It becomes the basis for judging the character of kings and the ultimate success or failure of their reigns.

As we have seen in the previous chapter, Moses' successor, Joshua, leads the second generation through a community-wide renewal of the covenant that their parents had made at Mount Sinai. Again, we recall that before he ever calls upon that generation to serve the Lord, he meticulously rehearses the mighty acts of God's grace. Reviewing once more the opening verses of Joshua 24, we find that the word "I" stands out in an unmistakable way: "I took your father Abraham. . . . I gave him Isaac. . . . I gave Esau the hill country . . . . I sent Moses and Aaron. . . . I plagued Egypt. . . . I brought you out. . . . I brought you to the land. . . . I handed them over to you. . . . I rescued you out of [Balaam's] hand. . . . I handed [the nations] over to you" (vv. 3-11). Then, once again we observe that Joshua reaches a crescendo of God's gracious faithfulness in verse 13 with these words: "I gave you a land on which you had not labored, and towns that you had not built, and you live in them; you eat the fruit of vineyards and oliveyards that you did not plant." Indeed, the Lord is the Deliverer who brought them into the land and the Provider who gives nourishment.

In the light of the gracious fidelity of God toward his people, Joshua proceeds in verse 14 to call upon the people to revere the Lord by serving him in sincere loyalty. Just as in the Shema, the call is not merely for the people to serve the Lord but for them to serve him wholly or completely (*tamim*). This same word of wholeness appears centuries earlier in God's covenant challenge to Abraham in Genesis 17:1: "Walk in my presence and be whole [*tamim*]" (author's translation). While some Bibles translate the word *tamim* as "blameless" or "perfect," the term itself positively connotes the idea of *complete* or *whole* and negatively connotes the idea of *empty of all rivals.* For this reason, Joshua instructs the people to "throw out" any rivals to the Lord and to serve the Lord completely or wholly. Giving them clear options, however, Joshua also permits them—if they are "unwilling to serve the LORD"—to choose from the gods of their past or the gods of the popular culture in which they now live (Josh. 24:15).

As Joshua continues his challenge to the people, he hints at something in the nature of God that stands behind the divine call to undivided love. Many of our Bibles translate the word in verse 19 as "jealous." Jealousy is usually perceived today as a negative character trait; jealous people set their eyes on what others have and desire it for themselves. In the light of this popular understanding of jealousy, the word "jealous" is perhaps not fully adequate. The text is not describing God as jealous of what others have and wanting it for himself. Rather, it describes God as desiring what is already his. The people with whom the Lord shares covenant ("I will be your God, and you will be my people" [Lev. 26:12, NLT]) are already his covenant people. As a result, he desires that he truly be their God and that they authentically be his people. Perhaps a more adequate translation for the depiction of God here is the word "zealous." The Lord is zealous or passionate for those with whom he has entered into covenant relationship. The word expresses the Lord's deepest desire to fully have what already belongs to him. As the delivering, providing, covenanting God to his people, he refuses to be shared with other gods.

The thread of *wholeness* continues to weave its way through the story of God's people far beyond Moses and Joshua. In 1 Samuel 12, Samuel speaks to the people with language similar to that of Moses and Joshua. After recounting the way in which the Lord had graciously delivered the people and after contrasting the people's repeated lack of trust in the Lord's fidelity, Samuel challenges the people: "Do not turn aside from following the Lord, but *serve the Lord with all your heart*; and do not turn aside after useless things that cannot profit or save, for they are useless. . . . Only fear the Lord, and *serve him faithfully with all your heart*; for consider what great things he has done for you" (vv. 20-21, 24, emphasis added).

In the next generation, on his deathbed King David challenges his son Solomon: "Be strong, be courageous, and keep the charge of the Lord your God. . . . Then the Lord will establish his word that he spoke concerning me: 'If your heirs take heed to their way, *to walk before me in faithfulness with all their heart and with all their soul*, there shall not fail you a successor on the throne" (1 Kings 2:2-4, emphasis added). In like manner, upon the completion of the construction of the temple in Jerusalem, the Lord appears to King Solomon and says, "As for you, if you will walk before me, as David your father walked, *with integrity* [from *tamim*, "wholeness" or "completeness"] *of heart* and uprightness, doing according to all that I have commanded you, and keeping my statutes and my ordinances, then I will establish your royal throne over Israel forever" (9:4-5, emphasis added).

And who can forget the magnificent challenge given by Elijah at Mount Carmel? The very clear-cut choice that he gives to the people sounds strangely reminiscent of the choice given by Joshua in Joshua 24. Since the people of God have succumbed to the allurement of the worship of Baal, Elijah asks, "How long will you go limping with two different opinions?" He then adamantly declares, "If the LORD is God, follow him; but if Baal, then follow him" (1 Kings 18:21). In stark contrast to the people's insistence that they would indeed also follow the Lord at the time of Joshua (Josh. 24:16-18), at the time of Elijah the air of popular religion had so infiltrated the minds and practices of the people that they did not respond to the prophet with a single word. They simply remained silent (1 Kings 18:21).

Finally, almost functioning as a bookend to Israel's story that began with Joshua's challenge to serve the Lord in faithful sincerity, King Josiah carries out a covenant-renewal ceremony between the Lord and the people. In 2 Kings 23:1-3, Josiah reads the words of the book of the covenant to all of the people, both great and small. He then participates in a covenant with the Lord in which he commits "to follow the LORD . . . *with all his heart and all his soul*" (v. 3, emphasis added). In response to the king's actions, the people also join in the covenant.

Not only do different prophets and leaders of the people challenge their own generation toward the "wholeness of heart" first expressed in the Shema, but often the story of God and his covenant people evaluates leaders themselves in the light of the call to undivided loyalty. Whether the judgment is positive or negative, the text evaluates a king based on his total or complete devotion to the Lord. A brief snapshot of these judgments gives us an idea of just how central "wholeness of heart" is in the prophetic telling of the God plot:

Positive Judgments of Kings

- Asa: "The heart of Asa was true to the LORD all his days" (1 Kings 15:14).
- Jehoshaphat: "He walked in all the way of his father Asa; he did not turn aside from it, doing what was right in the sight of the LORD" (22:43).
- Josiah: "Before him there was no king like him, who turned to the LORD with all his heart, with all his soul, and with all his might, according to all the law of Moses; nor did any like him arise after him" (2 Kings 23:25).

Negative Judgments of Kings

- Solomon: "King Solomon loved many foreign women. . . . Solomon clung to these in love. . . . When Solomon was old, his wives turned away his heart after other gods; and his heart was not true [*shalom*, "whole" or "undivided"] to the LORD his God" (1 Kings 11:1-2, 4).
- Abijam: "His heart was not true to the LORD his God, like the heart of his father David" (15:3).

This same concern for unadulterated fidelity to the Lord continues into the very heart of Jesus' Sermon on the Mount as he announces that no human being or community can serve two masters. In the words of Jesus, "A slave will either hate the one and love the other, or be devoted to the one and despise the other" (Matt. 6:24). From Jesus' perspective, it is not even possible for a human being to serve this uniquely (holy), gracious covenant God while also serving alternative sources of life, fertility, and hope (i.e., "mammon" [KJV], "money" [NIV], "wealth" [NRSV]). Jesus' adamant pronouncement allows no room for double-minded service: "You cannot serve God and wealth" (v. 24). Earlier in the same sermon, Jesus pronounces a blessing upon those persons whose minds are single focused and unmixed in their devotion. He describes them as "pure [i.e., "uncontaminated," "whole"] in heart"; they are the ones, according to Jesus, who will "see God" (5:8).

Centuries earlier, the worshipper in Psalm 24 raises the question concerning who is permitted to "ascend the hill of the LORD" and "seek the face of the God of Jacob" (vv. 3, 6). The response is given: "Those who have clean hands and *pure hearts*, who do not lift up their souls to what is false, and do not swear deceitfully" (v. 4, emphasis added). Similarly to Jesus bestowing his blessing upon the "pure in heart," the psalmist concludes that those with such untainted minds (*leb*) will be receiving "blessing from the LORD" (v. 5). Just as a pure metal is untainted with any alloy, so the pure heart/mind (*leb*) is unsullied with mixed loyalties. Indeed, the conviction behind Jesus' teaching concerning the "pure in heart" and the psalmist who ascends the "hill of the LORD" to worship is expressed through the memorable title of the book by nineteenth-century Danish philosopher Søren Kierkegaard: *Purity of Heart Is to Will One Thing.*[1]

three

DILEMMA
HOLY HILLS, SACRED COWS, AND SUBSTITUTE KINGS

WITHIN the unfolding God plot, the call to undivided fidelity occurs solely within the context of God's gracious activity. He never calls for complete devotion, untainted love, outside of deliverance, provision, and covenant. In fact, the call would not even make sense outside of God's preceding grace.

However, the realities of life, both then and now, seem to quickly overshadow this call to unadulterated fidelity to this unique (holy) covenant-making God. Very soon the people of God realize, "Uh-oh! We have a problem—a covenant-threatening problem!" It is the perennial dilemma of the human race. We want to trust this God who has delivered; we really do desire to believe wholeheartedly this God who has provided. There is something deep in our hearts that wishes we could be the faithful partner on the other end of the covenant. But the covenant-threatening dilemma seems never to disappear. The cultures and societies in which we live provide diverse options for our trust. These options compete for our undivided loyalty. In the light of what will now unfold in the story of the Lord's relationship with his covenant people as recounted in our Scripture, it is legitimate to refer to these competing options as holy hills, sacred cows, and substitute kings. Let's take a look at them.

Holy Hills

As soon as our biblical ancestors entered into the land that God had promised them, they faced the hurdle that all too often tripped them in generation after generation. This obstacle vehemently confronted them just as it has done for all generations up to this very day. When we read the Bible, we often read about a god in the land of Canaan by the name of Baal. Earlier we explored the way different manifestations of Baal were located throughout the villages of Canaan. Because we all too quickly conclude that this deity was simply a figment of the Canaanites' primitive and naive imaginations, we quickly skip over the stories and messages concerning Baal. Perhaps we give an amusing nod and smile as we think to ourselves, "This is one of those odd, ancient ideas that we modern folk don't have to worry about anymore."

But before we move on too quickly, we need to see in the worship of Baal the mind-set that is as alive and well in our contemporary world as it has ever been. Perhaps, it is even more thriving and addictive in our contemporary world and popular practices of religion today than it was thousands of years ago. So what is this mind-set? As a fertility religion, baalism is concerned with one thing—results. To put it another way, fertility religion is concerned with making things happen and with making them happen big! It seeks to make certain that the rain will come, that the crops will grow, and that the cattle will have calves. Growth is the name of the game for fertility religions.

But why would people become so concerned with growth? Survival! We've got to survive. We've got to have food to eat and water to drink. Forget about a God who has provided manna, quail, and water in the wilderness. That was an old, sentimental story. This is the "real world" we are talking about now. If our family and communities are to have a future, if our society and economy are to thrive, if our church and other institutions are to have a tomorrow, we've got to play the game "just right." Otherwise our demise is certain. Is this conclusion not correct? At least that is what our popular culture tells us, and so it provides us the baals in which we can place our trust and the baal practices in which we can participate.

So what then in Canaan did the worship of Baal look like? Just as in every culture, the system had been around for centuries. It appeared to have proven itself again and again. The system had its own logic that made sense. It had developed habitual practices and symbolic fixtures to represent those practices. Every village had its *high place*. This holy hill stood elevated above other structures in the village in order to bring the activities of worship closer to the heavens. Certainly everyone knew, "The closer I get to the heavens, the more likely I am to influence the gods or god." On the hill, one was likely to find several symbolic representations that growth or fertility was associated with the worship that took place there. A green tree demonstrated that indeed this place was fertile. "Results" happened here!

A wooden pole (Asherah pole) reminded the worshipper that the female goddess Asherah was intricately involved in this whole process. A pile of stones (*massebah*) reminded the worshipper that the male deity Baal was likewise intricately involved in the process of giving life, blessing, and fertility.

In the worship of the male and female fertility deities, different acts of the worshippers would prod the gods along. Those acts would influence, even manipulate, the gods to act promptly and benevolently. We see some of the desperate attempts of worshippers to get these gods to act in Elijah's encounter with the prophets of Baal in 1 Kings 18:20-29. Remember the context? Drought had set in; fertility was nowhere; death and destruction abounded. As in any society and culture, mere survival became the focus of social, religious, political, and economic life. So what do you do when you are desperate for rain? What do you do when the land, the people, and the institutions you love are dying by the moment? You call on the fertility gods. But you do more than call out in prayer. You limp around the altar (v. 26). You cry out and cut yourself with swords and lances until blood gushes out all over you (v. 28). You rave on as long as you can (v. 29). Out of your desperate attempt to survive, you will go to any lengths to get the gods to act on your behalf.

While not mentioned specifically in the Elijah narrative, a very common practice in the popular fertility religions was to engage in a sexual act with one of the temple "prostitutes" (called *holy ones* in our biblical text). The desired outcome would be Baal and Asherah's engagement in the same act. As a result of their sexual act, fertility would abound. Drenching showers would fall; growth and vitality would spring up all around. Most importantly, the land, the people, and the institutions would continue to survive and perhaps even grow.

So does this mind-set with its accompanying practices sound all that odd? Not really. Expressions of fertility religions differ across time and across cultures, but the mind-set remains the same. That mind-set tells human beings, and particularly religious human beings, that there are practices that worshippers can do on earth that will manipulate the gods or the god in the heavens. As a result of this mind-set, the center of trust is no longer in the unique (holy) God who graciously delivers and provides but in our own practices and in a system or a god that can be manipulated by our practices.

Sometimes the practices in which the people of God engage are questionable attempts to strong-arm God and to manipulate people into a response that will bring greater resources, unparalleled growth, and certainly survival. At other times, however, those practices can be as grounded and good as giving alms, fasting, and participating in acts of mercy and service. Sometimes they are the most cherished expressions of worship in which we participate: singing a hymn, praying a prayer, offering our tithes, proclaiming the gospel, kneeling at an altar, and even eating a meal together. However, when even the good, cherished, and life-giving practices of our faith are viewed as means of magically manipulating or coercing God and people, they have crossed over into the arena of Baal worship.

In our desperate attempts to survive, we climb the holy hills. We ascend the mountaintops that emerge when pop religion mixes with pop culture to provide us with systems that ensure survival and promise growth. While these systems are usually political and economic, they often bring God into the mix. The popular religion of the day all too easily seduces the believer into forms of worship and religious practices that seek to manipulate both God and neighbor. From culture to culture, generation to generation, pop religion consistently seems to be a "best seller" in the marketplace of ideas.

Psalm 121 unexpectedly gives expression to this problem confronting God's people. On the surface, the first words of this psalm evoke images of worshipping God in his creation high amid majestic mountains, perhaps caressed by cool breezes and entranced by the sound of soothing waterfalls: "I lift up my eyes to the hills—from where will my help come?" (v. 1). Reading these words in such a picturesque setting would seem ideal. However, on closer inspection we discover that the psalmist likely had something else in mind.

Rather than thinking about forested mountains or the beauty of creation, the psalmist simply looked across the terrain of his village and saw the many options his society offered him as sources for life, deliverance, nourishment, and hope. He raised that opening question not in the sweet assurance brought about by the majesty and stability of God's creation. He raised it in the utter bewilderment and dismay of what his culture with its political, economic, and religious realities had to offer him. There were so many hills, so many options, so many systems, and so many gods that offered fertility, life, and hope. They offered deliverance, provision, even covenant. In the end, they all promised survival! Within that context, the psalmist cries out in utter desperation: "I lift up my eyes to the hills; which one of these hills is my true source of help?"

Perhaps the more legitimate setting for reading Psalm 121 is not the majestic mountains of God's creation but the murky, overwhelming valley of our society's answers to life. There in the valley, we find ourselves in the institutions that provide direct access to financial security and political stability; they promise a bigger, better, and more robust way to live. There in the valley, we discover all around us the power structures that motivate us to get ahead and climb to the top ranks of our families, communities, workplaces, and churches. We see the lecture halls, studios, and media that we can so easily access for the self-helps and complete makeovers that promise survival and vitality. There in the valley, we look up and see hill after hill of worship centers that proclaim a gospel of prosperity for this life and the promise of extra jewels in an eternal crown for the next— all for the price of one more dollar or two more hours of service. Throughout the valley we see ads for pills and potions to solve our personal problems, hear songs to make us forget reality, and glimpse high-tech gadgets to take care of everything else.

There are so many hills to climb. There are so many options, so many possibilities, and so many systems. There are so many gods that promise release from yesterday, fulfillment for today, and hope for tomorrow. Their alluring symbols invite us to climb toward them. Their loud, strangely enticing, almost addictive voices encourage us to ascend their slopes. And there in the valley of options we lift up our eyes to the hills that surround and almost suffocate us. With our fellow sojourners of the human race, we cry out in bewilderment and anxiety, "From where does my help come?"

And then the still small voice speaks, "My help comes from the LORD, who made heaven and earth" (v. 2). Then that still small voice grows in its intensity and conviction, "My help comes from the LORD. . . . The LORD is your *keeper.* . . . The LORD will *keep* you from all evil. . . . The LORD will *keep* your going out and your coming in from this time on and forevermore" (vv. 2, 5, 7-8, emphasis added).

The call to God's people is for them to respond to the gracious self-giving love of God with fidelity and undivided allegiance. However, the holy hills allure us to climb them and to find atop them sources that we can control and manipulate so that we can manufacture life, blessing, and fertility on our own. What a dilemma: we are called to trust but allured to manipulation.

Sacred Cows

As the people of God discover themselves in the God plot, the dilemma does not stop at the holy hills of pop culture and pop religion. The dilemma intensifies in the tendency to confine divine activity within boundaries that we establish. We seek to contain God within our own humanly contrived systems. Often we seek to confine God to the forms in which he has appeared and acted in the past.

When we are threatened by circumstances, when we can't see God at work, when we grow impatient, or when we are simply seeking familiarity, we tend to fashion systems or structures in which God can appear and act. We shape plastic, artificial forms in which we can fit God. It's almost as if we build a house for God so that he can stay safely inside until we need him. Then when we need him, we know just how he works. He becomes our genie in our self-made bottle; like magic, we can open the bottle at will, and out comes our divine genie whom we can now control and manipulate. How safe we feel to have him in his little bottle that we have designed. How secure we are to know that we have him right at our fingertips.

It did not take long before our ancestors found themselves shaping their first of many genie bottles for God. Perhaps a more appropriate biblical term would be "sacred cows" or "idols." Even while Moses was still in the process of completing the covenant between God and God's people, our ancestors grew impatient and weary and insisted that Aaron shape a sacred cow for them.

Often when we speak of sacred cows or *idols*, we are referring to "important things" with a meaning similar to the way we define a god (see our discussion in the previous chapter). We often even say things such as, "Her home is her idol" or "His job is his idol." We talk about "idolizing" an athlete or an entertainer. However, in the grand dilemma of the God plot as envisioned by the prophetic voice, idols go way beyond important things or highly esteemed people. In the God plot, an idol is the humanly contrived attempt to maintain some type of control over God. By means of an idol, our trust is ultimately more in our neatly developed system of control over God than it is in God himself. The God who is free to be God becomes trapped and even enslaved in our little self-constructed systems, whether they be religious, political, or economic. The system defines God; the system attempts to contain God. If we can manip-

commitment

ulate or control the system, we will be able to manipulate or control God.

What a dilemma: we are called to an unadulterated trust in a covenant God who *graciously* delivers and provides and who is free to act, yet we are seduced by, involved in, and ultimately addicted to the trap of building sacred cows—idols—that will place this graciously and freely acting God into a "box" that we can control at will.

Substitute Kings/Alliances

The dilemma intensifies all the more in the story of this unique (holy), gracious God and his covenanted people—a people who are grounded in grace and called to undivided trust but seduced by holy hills and sacred cows.

Our ancestors knew their story well; they could recite it with great ease. When Pharaoh's armies had trapped them from the west and the Red Sea had trapped them from the east, the Lord had made a way. He had rescued them from their oppressors, and he had brought them through the sea on dry land. In that moment of utter despair when they were surrounded by undeniable destruction, Moses made vividly clear to the people just what kind of God the Lord was: "Do not be afraid, stand firm, and see the deliverance that the Lord will accomplish for you today. . . The Lord will fight for you, and you have only to keep still" (Exod. 14:13-14). No wonder Moses could lead the people in this remarkable song of worship:

I will sing to the Lord, for he has triumphed gloriously;

horse and rider he has thrown into the sea.

The Lord is my strength and my might,

and he has become my salvation;

this is my God, and I will praise him,

    my father's God, and I will exalt him.

The LORD is a warrior;

    the LORD is his name. (15:1-3)

They witnessed it firsthand. This God would fight their battles. Indeed, he himself would deliver them from evil. The battle was not theirs to fight.

However, although the people were eyewitnesses to the Lord's deliverance, one of their most persistent dilemmas was the fear that they could not fight the battle. "We cannot overcome our threats! Who will fight our battles?" Fear of loss, annihilation, and defeat paralyzed them again and again. This same fear has threatened to paralyze every generation since.

Do you recall what happened to the people of the generation that saw the beauty and the bounty of God's Promised Land? When they saw the giants in the land, they thought the battle was theirs to fight and gave up. Remember their words: "We came to the land to which you sent us; it flows with milk and honey, and this is its fruit. Yet the people who live in the land are strong, and the towns are fortified and very large" (Num. 13:27-28). Perceiving they had to be the giant slayers, an entire generation remained in the wilderness. In contrast to this reaction from those who believed the battle against giants was up to them are the words of the shepherd boy David to the giant Goliath: "You come to me with sword and spear and javelin; but I come to you in the name of the LORD of hosts" (1 Sam. 17:45).

Well before they finally got a king, the people of God had toyed with the idea of having a king. After Gideon had successfully defeated the enemies and became a judge over

Israel, the people offered the office of king to him. However, Gideon's response provides the prophetic-Deuteronomic conviction that the battle is the Lord's: "I will not rule over you, and my son will not rule over you; the LORD will rule over you" (Judg. 8:23). However, when the pressure eventually became too great, the covenant people could not resist the enticement to have a king. They insisted to Samuel, "We are determined to have a king over us, so that we also may be like other nations, and that our king may govern us and go out before us and fight our battles" (1 Sam. 8:19-20). How ironic that their insistence on having a king came immediately after the ark of the covenant had successfully made its way back to the people *on its own* after it had been stolen by the Philistines (chaps. 5–6). If the reality of the people's desperate desire to survive were not so sad, the irony would almost be funny. The Lord was strong enough to ensure the ark returned without any help from the people, yet they still thought they needed a king other than the Lord—a "substitute king"—who would fight their battles for them.

Throughout the story of God's covenant people, those substitute kings engaged in a repeated activity that demonstrated their own inability to trust God completely. One might even say that the "substitute kings" found their own "substitutes" as they entered into alliances with other nations. In seasons of peace and prosperity, these alliances were simply treaties of mutual assistance: "You help us out, and we will help you out." King Solomon is notorious for his alliance with the Egyptians in order to get building materials for his temple. King Omri did the same. So it seems, on the one hand, in the "good times" of life, the covenant people consistently sought to have greater prosperity, power, and successes. To do so, they made alliances with other powers and systems to assist them in fighting losing battles or in building a kingdom and expanding power.

On the other hand, in seasons of threat or attack, out of desperation and panic, the people of God sought such alliances so that another king, nation, or army could bail them out of life-threatening situations. Once again, the need to hold on to their lives, to survive, to maintain what they had, or to acquire even more moved the people to look elsewhere for covenant partners who promised to deliver them from their enemies and to provide for them in their neediness. In such times, the covenant community did not seek to expand its empire; it simply sought to save its own skin.

Of all the alliances of this type, probably one of the most memorable is associated with the panic and indecision of Judah's King Ahaz (see Isa. 7). The armies of the northern kingdom of Israel and of its allied partner Syria had made their way down toward Jerusalem. At the same time, the mighty Assyrian army was poised, ready to attack any runt nation that dared to think it could raise its head against the giant empire. What a decision Ahaz now had to face. Where would he turn? Should he join the alliance of little nations? Should he double-cross those little nations and play into the hands of the mighty Assyrians? The threat coming from both directions threw Ahaz into a panic. Most kings would think exactly what Ahaz did: "I must survive, and it is up to me to ensure my little kingdom of Judah survives." As a descendant of King David, Ahaz was responsible for protecting the people of Judah. Paralyzed by fear and stricken with terror, Ahaz was desperate, but then into this discouraging situation stepped the prophet Isaiah.

The prophet boldly announces, "Take heed, be quiet, do not fear, and do not let your heart be faint because of these two smoldering stumps of firebrands" (v. 4). Poetically, the prophet declares, "If you do not stand firm in faith, you shall not stand at all" (v. 9).

Why does Isaiah believe so boldly that Ahaz should not allow the threat to terrorize him or fear to paralyze him? The answer to Isaiah's confidence can be summarized in one succinct word: *Immanuel*, or "God is with us" (vv. 9-16). According to Isaiah, to become paralyzed by survival-driven fear and subsequently to turn to substitute kings and alliances for salvation is to reject the Lord himself as king. Isaiah poetically would say that Ahaz had rejected the life-giving waters that flow ever so gently (see 8:6).

The classic prophetic-Deuteronomic voices of Hosea and Jeremiah also understand alliances as "substitute kings." Hosea depicts the covenant people as making treaties with the Assyrians and carrying oil down to the Egyptians (Hos. 12:1; see also 8:9). He describes them as an easily deceived, foolish dove "now calling to Egypt, now turning to Assyria" (7:11, NIV). Specifically pointing to the substitute kings that Israel had been making for centuries, whether those kings be Israelite or non-Israelite, Hosea concludes, "Where now is your king, that he may save you? Where in all your cities are your rulers, of whom you said, 'Give me a king and rulers'?" (13:10). Pointing to the covenant people's incessant alliances with the great empires of Egypt and Assyria, the prophet Jeremiah poignantly asks, "What then do you gain by going to Egypt, to drink the waters of the Nile? Or what do you gain by going to Assyria, to drink the waters of the Euphrates?" (Jer. 2:18).

No wonder Jeremiah would describe this tendency to construct "survival systems"—whether they be sacred cows, holy hills, substitute kings, or political alliances—as the ultimate rebellion against this unique (holy) God who graciously delivers, provides, and makes covenant. He vividly depicts this tendency of the people of God through the imaginative metaphor of the self-made but broken water system. The prophet bemoans, "My people have committed two evils: they have forsaken me, the fountain of living water, and dug out cisterns for themselves, cracked cisterns that can hold no water" (v. 13). What a remarkably memorable image! What people from the time of Jeremiah to today cannot see in their own generation the same tendency? Water that haphazardly flows out of the rocky ground is a wonderful sight when we are thirsty. But, honestly, who would not want to construct their own well to hold water? The next time thirst would come, the cistern builder would have a guaranteed, foolproof source of water.

Cistern building really does seem to make sense. However, the great irony of this image is the cracks that begin to appear in the well. According to the classic prophetic-Deuteronomic voice of Jeremiah, the dependable wells that we construct for ourselves—whether in the name of holy hills, sacred cows, substitute kings, or political alliances—will always end in failure. Like a mirage in the desert, they seem to hold water, but they are full of cracks. Although these self-made wells initially create the illusion of reliability, security, and certainty, the cracks eventually develop. The wells that we thought to be foolproof are anything but that. They leak, grow weak, and crumble. Although we often are quite well aware of their fragile nature, we still believe that our own self-constructed, self-reliant wells are more trustworthy and reliable than a fountain of gushing water in which the best that we can do is hope, trust, and believe that it will continue to flow without our assistance or manipulation. All too often, our efforts to build wells for our own survival win out over simply receiving the gracious and free gift that emerges from outside of us.

So, honestly, what's the big deal about all these alliances? We do it every day, right? Nations make treaties with nations; businesses sell out and buy in with other businesses; and we sign contracts with builders, loan agents, and insurance companies regularly. What's going on with these alliances in the Bible? What's at stake?

Perhaps the best way we can describe a political alliance both *then* and *now* is as a power play. An alliance is a human endeavor to enter into a pact, a treaty, a *covenant,* with another individual or group of people who we consider to be more powerful than we are. We believe that this more powerful entity has the strength to protect, fight, nourish, and save us. We align ourselves with this entity in the false hope that we can save our own lives. We do it as the people of God—ancient Israel and the contemporary church—in relationship to governments, economic systems, and even pop culture itself. If we join these power holders—their way, their party, their line of thinking—we believe we can save our own skin. We may even be elevated to a position of higher status and greater power. What is ironic with all this is that a community that has already said "I do" to a divine covenant Partner who delivers and provides would now say "I do" to multiple other partners. Some would call this action polygamy. However, the prophetic-Deuteronomic voice—the voice of the prophets Hosea and Jeremiah—depicts such activity as infidelity or prostitution. Within the God plot, this unique (holy) covenant-making God had called and set apart a unique (holy) community. This community was not only to love its covenant God but to love him with an undivided love, an unadulterated fidelity, an entire devotement.

Some things just don't seem to change from generation to generation. In the midst of threats of our annihilation, fears that the best we can do is survive, and anxiety that God may not be as trustworthy as we would wish, we seek kings who will fight our battles and we seek alliances that will save us. Although cultures and systems differ across time and space, each culture offers its own kings and alliances. Popular political systems will fight our political enemies, popular economic systems will defeat our economic challenges, and yes, popular religious systems will guarantee our prosperity as well as our present and eternal survival.

At the Heart of the Dilemma

So centuries later, what are the holy hills, the sacred cows, the substitute kings, and the political alliances that present us with the dilemma the covenant people have always faced—that of maintaining an unadulterated trust in God? They take on different forms, shapes, and sizes from culture to culture and from era to era. However, when all is said and done, the sacred cows, holy hills, substitute kings, and life-saving alliances are only the tangible evidence or the symptoms of a much deeper dilemma within the minds/hearts of the people of God. This deeper dilemma is the dilemma of the human race. Beneath the surface of the holy hills, sacred cows, substitute kings, and alliances is the human struggle to trust. We might even say that we have a very real inclination toward mistrust. All the way back to Eden in Genesis 3, we hear the appeal to our mistrust: "Did God really say you will die? Surely, you will not die!" (v. 4, author's translation). Can we really trust this God?

In discussing Adam and Eve's action in the garden of Eden, Old Testament scholar Terence Fretheim has poignantly described the very essence of the human dilemma as a mistrust of God. He defines the first sin as a "mistrust of God and God's word, which then manifests itself in disobedience and other negative behaviors."[1]

However, there is something even below the surface of our mistrust of God. That reality can be summarized in a single word: "fear." This fear that gives birth to our mistrust of God emerges from something even deeper within the human psyche: our desire for survival. When the survival of our lives, societies, families, and institutions is threatened, we become terrified. Faced with the prospects of death, loss, defeat, and humiliation, we seek whatever might save us. We seek religious, political, and economic systems—hills that we can climb, on which we can perform well, and through which we can gain the fertility promised. We seek to encapsulate divine power (God/gods) according to how that divine power has once appeared in our lives. We then proceed to construct idols we can manipulate and control or, at least, think we can manipulate and control. We seek kings/systems that have proven they can fight our enemies. They surely can overcome our threat of annihilation and assure our survival.

When survival becomes our reason for existence, we can be certain that our demise is imminent. When survival becomes the goal and motivation for an individual, a community, a nation, and certainly the church itself, the spiral toward destruction has begun. No one has described this reality more clearly than Jesus in his words to his disciples, who will struggle repeatedly with the survival issue: "If any want to become my followers, let them deny themselves and take up their cross and follow me. For those who want to save their life will lose it, and those who lose their life for my sake, and for the sake of the gospel, will save it. For what will it profit them to gain the whole world and forfeit their life?" (Mark 8:34-36). What a haunting question: What profit is there in your survival if you lose your very reason for being? Walter Brueggemann has insightfully commented about the fear that so often cripples and paralyzes the people of God:

> In these days, fear is deep and broad in the land and in the church. Fear does strange things to people. It makes us withdraw from our brothers and sisters and live in a crouch. It makes us attracted to a fetal position. It makes us say things and do things that do not honor us. It makes us hurt one another—all because we fear the world is falling apart. Fear is our modern form of atheism, fear that there is no order but the one I invent. Thus, I must protect what little order I have, scramble to make more, and keep people from intruding on my order or my mystery or my goodies, because if they come there, it will all fall apart. There is no one but me, and I must hustle.[2]

Holy hills, sacred cows, and substitute kings—they are only the tip of the iceberg. Far beneath the surface of the systems we climb in our search for blessing, deep within the idols we construct and bow to daily, and far beyond the kings we call upon to fight our battles is the very pulse of the human dilemma: out of our fear of loss emerging from our insistence upon survival, we just cannot trust the gracious God who delivers and provides. We mistrust this One who covenants with us, "I will be your God, and you will be my people" (Lev. 26:12, NLT). We want to trust. We want to believe. We wish we could say "Amen" not only with our lips but also with our minds/hearts. However, this struggle is the human struggle. This battle is the human battle. This dilemma is not simply the dilemma of rebellious and evil people but the story of people. It is the struggle of the covenant people of God because they are people.

So what are we to do? If this is the human dilemma, are we stuck? Are we called to an undivided loyalty to this gracious covenant-making God only to fall repeatedly to the human dilemma of mistrust? Will we forever climb holy hills and continue to build one more sacred cow after another? Are substitute kings and alliances simply the way it will always be? Have we now written "the end" on the God plot? In the next chapter we will look again at this dilemma and explore whether there is a way to resolve it and, if so, what that resolution might be.

four

RESOLUTION
REVIVE US AGAIN...
AND AGAIN...AND AGAIN?

WE HAVE COME to a predicament in the God plot that seems unresolvable—the dilemma of mistrust. This dilemma is all too human and expresses itself in a failure to trust God that arises out of a fear for survival. So, is there any answer to this human dilemma as it is faced by the covenant people? Is there any hope? Is there any resolution? Perhaps the familiar phrase (or excuse) is the final answer: "Well, I'm only human. I'm only flesh and blood." Or does the prophetic voice give us a different answer to this roadblock in the plot of God?

A Long Line of "Returns":
Connecting the Dots

Without question, the prophets sought an answer to this perennial dilemma of holy hills, sacred cows, and substitute kings. Much of what the prophetic voice addresses is directly related to this very matter. Indeed, if there were "covenant police" among our biblical ancestors, they would have been the prophets. Perhaps this popular adage fittingly describes the prophetic search for resolution: "If at first you don't succeed, try, try again!" The Avis rental car motto expresses the prophetic attempt at resolution even better: "We try harder." Or maybe we should just let the prophets speak for themselves through the single word they repeatedly employed: *shub*, meaning "return," "repent," or "turn back." As examples of this familiar prophetic call, take a look at Jeremiah 3:12, 14, 22; 4:1; 18:11; Ezekiel 14:6; 18:30; Hosea 14:1-2; Joel 2:12-13; Zechariah 1:3-4; Malachi 3:7. From these scriptures we can discern that the prophets' centuries-old answer to the dilemma facing humanity is, "Turn back . . . again! Repent . . . again!"

The subplot of a perpetual turning away from God and then back to God through a series of community revivals begins as early as the covenant-renewal ceremony in Joshua 24. In this ceremony, as we have previously observed, Joshua echoes Moses' earlier call of the Shema as he challenges the people: "Put away the gods that your ancestors served . . . and serve the LORD. . . . choose this day whom you will serve. . . . but as for me and my household, we will serve the LORD" (vv. 14-15). Sure enough, the people immediately and insistently respond, "Far be it from us that we should forsake the LORD to serve other gods. . . . we also will serve the LORD, for he is our God" (vv. 16, 18). Ironically, Joshua is well aware of the repeated struggle the people will have to trust the Lord completely as he responds, "You cannot serve the LORD, for he is a holy God" (v. 19). What? He first calls them to be undividedly loyal to God only to tell them that they can't? So will the plot of God end in a dead end? Is God really calling his people to do the impossible?

Very similar to Joshua's call, two centuries later Samuel, in his farewell address, boldly challenges the Israelites to an undivided loyalty and trust (1 Sam. 12). After rehearsing the many faithful acts of the Lord to his people, along with the people's habitual mistrust, Samuel calls upon the people and their king to "fear the LORD and serve him and heed his voice and not rebel against the commandment of the LORD" (v. 14) and to "serve the LORD with *all your heart*" and "not turn aside after useless things that cannot profit or save" (vv. 20-21, emphasis added). Yet in spite of his challenging words, the dilemma will continue to persist in the life of the covenant people.

Again, very similar to the challenges of both Joshua and Samuel, King David's final words to his successor Solomon call for undivided loyalty and trust in the Lord. David first challenges his son to "be strong, be courageous, and keep the charge of the LORD your God, walking in his ways and keeping his statutes" (1 Kings 2:2-3). He then proceeds to describe the manner in which Solomon and the subsequent heirs to the throne are to walk with the Lord: "in faithfulness with *all their heart* and with *all their soul*" (v. 4, emphasis added). After Solomon completes the construction of the temple and his own palace, the Lord promises that a Davidic successor to the throne will forever continue if he will walk before the Lord "with *integrity* [*tam*, from *tamim*, "wholeness," "completeness"; see discussion of Josh. 24:19 in chap. 2 above] *of heart* and uprightness, doing according to all that I have commanded you" (1 Kings 9:4, emphasis added). At the dedication of the temple in Jerusalem, even Solomon himself declares to the people, "Devote yourselves *completely* [from *shalom*, "whole," "complete"] to the LORD our God, walking in his statutes and keeping his commandments" (8:61, emphasis added). Yet in spite of David's challenge, the Lord's admonition, and Solomon's own words, the Scriptures summarize the end of Solomon's reign with this description: "When Solomon was old, his wives turned away his heart after other gods; and his heart was not true [*shalom*, "whole," "complete"] to the LORD his God" (11:4).

A well-remembered hallmark of the many revivals of God's people is the revival in the ninth century BC under the leadership and inspiration of the prophet Elijah. Do you remember the dramatic way this revival begins? In an "in your face" manner, Elijah confronts the pop religion of the day. He presents a direct challenge to the fertility religion of baalism. As we described earlier, this pop religion sought to bring about self-made blessings through the worship of Baal. In its almost magical search for rain, it guaranteed the results of worship. So what does Elijah do at the outset of his revival? He proclaims the onset of a drought, not in the name of the pop fertility god, Baal, but in the name of the covenant-making God, Yahweh. Eventually that action takes him to Mount Carmel, where he poses the question that we vividly remember almost three thousand years later: "How long will you go limping with two different opinions? If the LORD is God, follow him; but if Baal, then follow him" (18:21). Only the prophet who truly knows the Source of fertility would first proclaim a drought. Only the prophet who truly understands who the Supplier of nourishing and refreshing waters is could pour out precious water all around the altar of sacrifice.

After Elijah's memorable victory over the prophets of Baal at Mount Carmel, the first of a series of revivals among God's people in the prophetic history (Joshua–2 Kings) begins swiftly. The Baal prophets are removed. Actually they are destroyed. Talk about getting rid of all that stands in the way of God's people having an authentic walk with God. How much more serious could you get? However, the revival, along with the deep commitment to ridding the land of all rivals to the Lord, actually goes into overdrive after Elijah. This revival does not stop simply by ridding the land of all of the prophets and prophetesses of Baal. Once a new revival-oriented king, Jehu, is in place, he almost seems to go crazy over the revival (see 2 Kings 9–10)! He puts Elijah's anti-Baal, pro-Yahweh revival on steroids, driving his chariot like a madman (where we get the catchphrase "driving like an old Jehu") to get to Ahab and Jezebel's palace. Remember, it was Ahab under the influence of his wife, Jezebel, who led the people into the pop religion of baalism.

After being cast from the palace tower, Jezebel crashes to the ground, and the dogs lick up her blood. Okay, so the story is graphic; actually, the story is quite horrific! But in all of its gory character, it attempts to make the point that this revival is serious. This revival is laying it all down. It seeks to demolish every idol and to remove the very sources of the problem contaminating the kingdom: Ahab, Jezebel, the prophets of Baal, and the Baal temple. Then when it seems as if the revival could not get any more serious, it makes a final move in its destruction of all that opposes the people's wholehearted fidelity toward the Lord. After leading the people through an incredible tearing down of Baal altars and a remarkable refurbishment of the Lord's altar, Jehu turns the Baal sanctuary into a public toilet. The biblical text speaks for itself: "They brought out the pillar that was in the temple of Baal, and burned it. Then they demolished the pillar of Baal, and destroyed the temple of Baal, and made it a latrine to this day. Thus Jehu wiped out Baal from Israel" (10:26-28).

Talk about serious results! Just imagine what the newspaper headline of that revival would have been: "Mighty Revival Results in Temple Becoming Public Toilet!" Indeed, any witness to this revival would have deemed it an absolute success—a revival to brag about for decades to come and one that every other village would have wanted to duplicate and repeat!

Unfortunately, although Jehu might have wiped out the worship of Baal from Israel, in a matter of no time, the people were right back to their same old ways. In fact, not many decades later the prophet Hosea, speaking to the same nation where Elijah's revival occurred, vividly depicts through his marriage to a prostitute named Gomer the covenant people's unfaithfulness to the Lord. Hosea describes the situation of the people in this way: "A spirit of whoredom has led them astray, and they have played the whore, forsaking their God. They sacrifice on the tops of the mountains, and make offerings upon the hills, under oak, poplar, and terebinth, because their shade is good" (Hos. 4:12-13). Depicting the people as "joined to idols" (v. 17), Hosea portrays the ways they love to make sacrifices and give offerings in worship (8:11; 10:1). However, the Lord announces, "I desire steadfast love [covenant faithfulness] and not sacrifice, the knowledge of God rather than burnt offerings" (6:6).

So what happened to Elijah's and Jehu's mighty revival? Were the people just not sincere enough? Perhaps they didn't really mean it when they burned up the Baal altar and turned it into a public toilet. Maybe they were only acting as though they were giving up the other gods to serve the Lord. When we look at the entire picture, can we really be sure that the revival under Jehu was as mighty and far reaching as the text describes it? If we carefully take into account the plotline of the relationship between the Lord and his covenant people, we can confidently answer, "Yes! The revival was absolutely far reaching and widespread. Yes! They genuinely and sincerely meant to be undividedly the Lord's. Yes! They burned everything contrary to God, abandoned false gods over to a public latrine, and reestablished their worship of the Lord alone. Yes! It was a mighty revival, just as the text describes."

Having mighty revivals, laying it all down on the altar, burning the competing altars, and establishing far-reaching reforms are all great. They do good things in the life of God's people. But if we are honest with the plot of God and his covenant people, simply "trying harder," "giving up more," or "burning down every idol" is just not the final answer to the dilemma. It's good, important, and has value, but it does not change the dilemma God's people face with the ultimate divine call in the God plot: "Love the LORD your God with *all* . . ." (Deut. 6:5, emphasis added). We can throw evil Jezebel out the window and burn the temple of the Lord's dominant competition, but the problem remains. Such actions, as good and well-meaning as they may be, became for the covenant people then and become for the covenant people now something similar to pulling weeds out of a garden. You can take care of all of the symptoms, but the weeds just keep returning. And so they did for our ancestors!

Not long after Jehu's far-reaching revival in the northern kingdom, the southern kingdom also had a thoroughgoing reform. We read about this revival in 2 Kings 11–12. Ironically, Jezebel's daughter, Athaliah, had married into David's royal family down in the southern kingdom. Indeed, in this situation, it was "like mother, like daughter." Under Athaliah's Baal-oriented rule, the people of Judah did exactly what the people of Israel had done. They abandoned their undivided, wholehearted loyalty to the Lord and began to climb their own holy hills and build their own sacred cows. However, while Athaliah attempted to wipe out any future Davidic king from Judah, young Joash was hidden and trained in the *torah* of the Lord by the priest Jehoiada. When Joash was seven years old, a great revolution took place in Judah. After having Athaliah overthrown and killed, the priest Jehoiada led the people of God into a remarkable, memorable revival. A genuine covenant-renewal service took place once again between the people and their covenant God. Once the service was over, the renewed people responded. They went to the temple of Baal, tore it apart, shattered all the altars and idols of Baal, and killed the leading priest of the temple.

Placed upon the throne, young King Joash oversaw a major and thoroughgoing repair of the Lord's temple. The revival was comprehensive and authentic. But just as the revival in the northern kingdom was, this revival also lasted only a short time. The people returned to their old ways. Burned altars, demolished idols, assassinated priests, overthrown queens, rededicated temples—you really would think that such changes would take care of the problem. And they did—for a while. But as thoroughgoing and extensive as the revival was, the teaching ministry of Jehoiada and the leadership of young Joash had no permanence.

Although almost three thousand years separate us from these events, we can see ourselves, our churches, and our popular Christian faith reflected in them. We have seen prophetic ministry at work in our worship services during remarkable times of renewal and reform. We have watched idols being demolished and temples of false gods burned. We have celebrated the giving of genuine promises to God and neighbor and the making of sincere commitments. But then a week, a month, or a year later, we have also seen the reemergence of plastic idols, both old and new. We have witnessed the reappearance of alliances with substitute kings to "save our own skin." We have observed the rebuilding of Baal temples and the reestablishment of Asherah altars. And then amid all these occurrences we have asked ourselves, "So was our commitment real? Were our promises sincere? Or was it all a charade?" More than likely, our answer is usually, "Our commitment was indeed genuine; our promises were truly sincere. There was no charade. We have destroyed altars, temples, and idols. We have given up everything to God. We have rebuilt his sanctuary and reestablished his altar." Yet regardless of the generation, the culture, or the Christian tradition to which we belong, we find ourselves again and again in that pesky but familiar "fidelity, infidelity; wholehearted, halfhearted" cycle.

Is there any hope? Are we stuck? The human dilemma hovers over us once again, and the shadow of despair almost convinces us that the God plot has met its end. Unfortunately, for some of us the cycle has so repeated itself that we have indeed concluded that the call to undivided love and trust is not possible. The God plot has met its end. There is no resolution—or perhaps the resolution is the reality of no resolution?

As the story of this covenant God and his covenant people continues to unfold, just a few generations after both Elijah/Jehu and Jehoiada/Joash, another great revival among God's people takes place. In fact, if it is possible, this revival may have even exceeded both Jehu's and Joash's together. The leader was good King Hezekiah. The revival was undoubtedly one of the most sweeping, life-changing events in the covenant community's history. We read about this revival in 2 Kings 18. It is an understatement to say that the event was memorable. This revival was so mighty that not only were evil things destroyed, but even the good things that had become corrupted were demolished. No doubt, the northern kingdom of Israel had become an object lesson for the people in the southern kingdom. By now, the northern kingdom of Israel had fallen to Assyria. The invincible kingdom of Israel that had been fortified with mighty towers, built upon alliances with great nations, and led by clever kings was no more. The warnings and the multiple calls to repentance by prophets such as Elijah, Amos, and Hosea undoubtedly echoed far beyond their original northern audience. Their words had a ripple effect as they spoke into the life of the covenant people in the south. This community must have concluded, "If it happened to them, it surely could happen to us as well!"

With the vivid living example of her northern sister in the background, the stage was set for a great revival in the south. Not only did King Hezekiah get rid of all of the temples of other gods, demolish the altars, and obliterate the idols, but he also went a step further. Do you recall the time in the wilderness when the people were bitten by snakes? Moses constructed a copper serpent—later named Nehushtan. As the people gazed upon it, they were healed (Num. 21:8-9). Looking back on that event in the life of God's people, we could say now that the copper serpent was a means of God's grace for the people. In the wilderness, the serpent did not function as a means to manipulate God but as a means to focus upon the God who could freely restore them to health. Nehushtan was not the healer; the Lord God was the Healer. The generation in the wilderness knew this reality quite well. However, over many centuries, this instrument of God's grace had become an idol for the people. Rather than trusting the God to which the copper serpent pointed, the people had come to put their trust in the copper serpent itself. The copper serpent had not changed, but the people's understanding and use of it in their worship had changed. An instrument of divine grace had become an instrument to manipulate the divine.

This "copper serpent syndrome" seems to repeat itself from generation to generation. Each generation, sometimes unwittingly and sometimes more purposefully, tends to take the good gifts of God, the instruments of grace he has given, and places trust in them rather than in God. So what did Hezekiah do about the copper serpent? Certainly his response was drastic! His revival was so deep and wide, so prevailing, that he did not simply "reform" the copper serpent; he demolished it. Nevertheless, in spite of Hezekiah's sincere and thoroughgoing revival, in no time at all, the people were once again climbing holy hills, building sacred cows, and seeking refuge from kings and security from alliances.

So once more in the story of God's interaction with his covenant people, we see the "fidelity, infidelity" cycle repeating itself. Amid all their sincere reforms, well-meaning revivals, and authentic covenant renewals, the people of God really could have borrowed that Avis rental car motto mentioned earlier: "We try harder!" But apparently responses such as trying harder, committing more, and giving up more do not solve the dilemma. Is there hope? Are we stuck?

Finally we arrive at the reform that surpassed all reforms in the story of God's people. If any reform would solve the problem and allow the plot of God with his covenant people to finally reach resolution, this one would surely do so. If the time had ever been just right for the people to undergo a complete, thoroughgoing reformation, this time was it. We read about this revival in 2 Kings 22–23.

Firmly in place as king, Josiah had ruled over Judah for eighteen years. The mighty power of Assyria was waning significantly, and Babylon had not yet arrived at its immense power. In the midst of this power vacuum, King Josiah had greater liberties to pursue his own agenda. Josiah insisted that with the money that had come into the temple treasury, the high priest Hilkiah purchase timber and stone and pay carpenters and stonemasons to repair the temple. In the midst of the temple repairs, Hilkiah reported that the *torah* of Moses had been discovered in one of the storage rooms of the temple. After consulting Huldah the prophetess on the authenticity of this discovery, Josiah went up to the temple, read the book of the covenant publicly, and led the entire nation through a covenant renewal. Both king and people agreed to carefully follow all that was read.

As a result of the declaration of both Josiah and the people to follow the Lord completely, unparalleled responses followed. The people of God had never experienced such an amazing reform. From all appearances, it was absolutely genuine. The Scripture's depiction of the utter destruction and abandonment of all that stood in opposition to the Lord God is unmatched throughout the Bible. All vessels constructed for Baal and Asherah were burned. Idolatrous priests were removed from office. The image of the fertility goddess Asherah was burned and beat to dust; the dust was thrown upon graves. All the holy hills were desecrated and destroyed. The atrocious practice of child sacrifice stopped. Images of horses often used in the worship of the sun were shattered. Altars to other gods were decimated, and Asherah poles were destroyed and covered with human bones. The list goes on and on: Josiah stamped out wizards and mediums and household gods (*teraphim*) and idols.

Do you have a sense of what this revival was really like? Undoubtedly we would use words such as "amazing," "remarkable," "awesome," and "memorable." Those words are understatements to say the least. Josiah's reform was indeed the "dream revival" of every church, every pastor, every lay leader, and every denomination! It was sincere. It is one thing to forsake other gods and their worship sites. However, in this case, gods and temples were not only forsaken but destroyed.

This revival was so authentic and thoroughgoing that even the rival worship site at Bethel (yes, the site where Jacob dreamed of heavenly messengers descending and ascending on the heavenly staircase [see Gen. 28]) was destroyed. This revival was so determined to never turn back from absolute fidelity to the Lord God that Jerusalem became the sole place of worship. In limiting the worship site to Jerusalem, the pop theology of the culture in the villages and towns would never again contaminate the people. What a way to keep an eye on the situation! Finally, the grand climax to this mighty revival occurred as the people celebrated the Festival of Passover in an appropriate way—something that had not occurred since the days of the judges. No wonder the writer of Josiah's life made this conclusion about the king who led such a mighty, far-sweeping revival: "Before him there was no king like him, who turned to the LORD with all his heart, with all his soul, and with all his might, according to all the law [torah] of Moses; nor did any like him arise after him" (2 Kings 23:25).

Under Josiah's reform, the people would not simply have the slogan "We try harder!" Indeed, they would have had the slogan "We try the hardest!" Unfortunately, just as we have seen in the preceding remarkable revivals, trying harder, committing more, and giving up more didn't resolve the dilemma. One more time, as we read the plot of this unique (holy) God in covenant with his people, we are moved to ask, "Is there hope? Are we stuck?"

Prophetic Disillusionment over Reform/ Revival/Renewal

So let's rehearse what we have seen so far. If we connect the dots within the God plot, one revival follows another. Now don't misunderstand what the God plot is saying. In no way is it making light of the numerous and popular attempts throughout history to reform, revive, and renew the life of God's people. There have always been and always will be meaningful and significant places and times for renewing our covenant with the Lord, opening our lives to his fresh work, and being reminded of who we are as his people. God's people have always known that it is just far too easy to forget the gracious activity of God and likewise to forget who we are as people in covenant with him. We desperately need intentional seasons of rehearsing, renewing, and replenishing our identity as the covenant community.

However, we've got to be honest with the pattern of the God plot found in Scripture. The pattern is clear: one generation gives everything up to God, but even before that generation dies, the people of God return to climbing holy hills to be nourished, rebuilding sacred cows to contain God, depending upon their substitute kings to fight their battles, and allying with the surrounding culture to survive.

By connecting the dots in the plot of the God who is in covenant with his people, we come to find that in spite of all the efforts to renew, to change, to make the definitive decision "this time" to be people of wholehearted fidelity, each reform falls short. Again, we might conclude, "Well, they just weren't serious enough." But from every indication in Scripture, they were very serious. They were very genuine. There was something else at stake. The issue went much deeper than committing a little more or a whole lot more to God. Something even broader, deeper, and wider than sincere commitment was at stake.

Toward the end of all of these reforms and revivals, the prophet Jeremiah seems to have finally begun to connect the dots. He saw the situation both in his own day and across the preceding generations for exactly what it was. Jeremiah was likely an active supporter of the great reform of King Josiah. All one has to do is read his oracles in Jeremiah 3–4 to see his numerous calls for the people to *shub*, to repent or turn back around. He makes the same call that prophets before him had made. In Jeremiah 2:22, he utters a classically prophetic call using the "turning word," *shub*, three times: *"Turn, O turning children, and I will heal your turning"* (author's translation).

Possibly during the revival of Josiah, Jeremiah uses a vivid and memorable image—one that was introduced in the previous chapter—to describe the ongoing dilemma of the people of God as they forsake their covenant God to seek out systems they can control (see 2:13). As you may recall, Jeremiah depicts the people forsaking the Fountain of living/flowing water in favor of constructing their own cisterns to contain their water. Again, the process of building cisterns makes sense. Who wouldn't want to build up their own reservoir of water to which they could turn whenever thirsty? Having to depend (or should we say trust?) that a flowing fountain would keep on supplying water in times of thirst is too risky. The certainty of having a cistern always seems to be better than depending on another source of water that perhaps could dry up. An ardent supporter in the early days of Josiah's revival, Jeremiah likely uses the image of turning to self-made cisterns to describe the perennial dilemma of the people in climbing holy hills, constructing sacred cows, and turning to substitute kings.

However, as time passes and the covenant people increasingly come to see the Jerusalem temple as a human construction in which they can place their trust (see Jer.

7, 26), Jeremiah begins to recognize the futility of simply "shubbing," or turning back, to God. While we may turn to the Lord on one day or in one season, we just have this habit of turning to another system that promises life and fertility on the next day or in the subsequent season. Perceiving the way people fall right back into their old ways, Jeremiah holds nothing back in his description of the addictive nature of holy hills, sacred cows, and substitute kings. He depicts the people habitually turning to other sources of deliverance and provision as wild animals in heat as they lust for their mate (see 2:23-24). Quoting the people themselves, Jeremiah exclaims, "It is hopeless, for I have loved strangers, and after them I will go" (v. 25).

As if to throw his hands in the air and give up on the people, the prophet exclaims, "Can Ethiopians change their skin or leopards their spots? Then also you can do good who are accustomed to do evil" (13:23). In other words, these people just can't change their ways. The inability to trust the Lord wholeheartedly seems to be engrained in the very nature of who they are. No matter how hard they try, how many idols they burn, or how many yeses they say to God, it just seems that there is no escape from climbing holy hills, constructing sacred cows, and setting up substitute kings.

Jeremiah takes this desperate, hopeless situation to an even deeper level when he moves beyond the actions of the people to describe their *leb* (see meaning of the *leb* as the "heart/mind" in our discussion of the Shema in chap. 2). He describes the heart as more "devious," "perverse," and impossible to "understand" than anything else (17:9). He graphically depicts the way the people's sin ("missing the mark") is "engraved" on their hearts with an iron pen and a "diamond point" (v. 1). It is etched on their very minds. No wonder they act the way they do. They behave in certain ways because they *think* in certain ways. In other words, they could wear WWJD (What Would Jesus Do?) bracelets around their wrists every moment of every day, but if their hearts/minds/thought processes are perverse, then their actions are bound to be perverse or, at least eventually, will be perverse. Reform, revival, and renewal can only go so far in changing behavior. They work for at least a while. However, Jeremiah becomes absolutely convinced that behavioral reform is only temporary. There is more than actions at stake; the heart/mind (*leb*) is at stake. Changing a person's actions does not change his or her mind. Strong determination goes a long way to improve a person's actions, but strong determination cannot change the very way he or she thinks.

In the depths of his insight, Jeremiah saw something that believers all too easily overlook. This is just the way humans are: they struggle to trust, and they often mistrust. Or perhaps in better words, we humans just have the propensity, the leaning, toward finding our own ways to deliver ourselves and to provide for ourselves. Engendered by our survival-oriented mind-set and the accompanying fear that we will not survive, we find it simpler and much less complicated to trust ourselves. If not ourselves, we at least lean into trusting the religious systems and practices we can devise and the economic and political systems and practices we can manipulate and control. What this all boils down to is a mind-set of fear-driven, survival-oriented mistrust of the gracious covenant-making God who delivers and provides—the great dilemma to the God plot. God calls his people to complete love, unadulterated fidelity, and wholehearted trust, while the people's hearts/minds (*leb*) are bound to be divided. It's just the way they are!

Is That All?

So we can no more change our ways than Ethiopians can change the color of their skin or than leopards can remove their spots? Is that it? Is that the final answer? So God calls, but we can't—is that the end of the story? More than a roadblock to the God plot, if this is the final answer, the God plot is at a dead end! So do we conclude that God has called his people—both then and now—to a grand ideal, to the ideal of loving him with all of our heart, all of our soul, and all of our strength, but that it is an ideal that will never take place?

Perhaps we fall into the same trap that many believers do. Maybe our conclusion as believers in Jesus Christ is as follows: "Since we are unable to love the Lord with wholehearted allegiance, the love of God as expressed through the person of Jesus Christ is God's way of covering his eyes so that he does not see our inability or unwillingness to love him without rival." But what kind of God is that? What kind of God would play mind games with himself? What kind of God calls the people with whom he shares covenant to wholehearted allegiance only to "psych" himself into an alternative reality that doesn't exist? We at least have to be honest about that kind of answer! At the most, it paints a picture of a weak God, and at the least, it depicts a God deluding himself about a people who cannot wholeheartedly love him.

Perhaps we could go another direction. It may sound something like the following: "When God looks upon his people who can no more change their ways than a leopard remove its spots, he now sees the one human who demonstrated undivided love and complete trust in the Father—the Son, Jesus Christ." We might imagine that somehow the Father has placed the Son between us and himself so that the love and surrender of the Son take the place of our inability or unwillingness to love God with complete loyalty. But wait! What kind of God is that? Is this response another quick fix—or should we say an artificial fix—to the human dilemma? In the end, it may give the Father a positive image to gaze at, but it leaves the human race and the covenant people unchanged. It may change God's view, but it doesn't change us.

This unique (holy) covenant God calls his covenant people to undivided loyalty, with the whole heart, whole soul, and whole strength. However, we seem to be as stuck as we ever were. We keep on climbing our holy hills, building our sacred cows, and calling out for our substitute kings!

Wow! Wretched, disabled, weak people that we are. Is there any hope? Can anything or anyone ever deliver us from this confounding human reality? Must we now simply conclude that it is hopeless? Does the God plot really reach a dead end?

Somewhere in the process of reading Jeremiah, we have stopped short. We heard him say that we can no more change our ways than leopards can remove their spots or than Ethiopians can change the pigment of their skin. We heard him say that sin is etched on our hearts with a diamond pen. But we stopped reading there. It is amazing what stopping short in a plot will do for the overall story. The reader will never reach the final resolution by stopping short at a text that is only intended to prod him or her along further. To stop short is like watching a murder mystery and then leaving just after a particular suspect has been ruled out. You have got to stay around long enough to see who the guilty culprit is, or else you will end up misinterpreting the mystery. How much more, then, when we stop short with the human dilemma—or for that matter, when we stop short in reading Jeremiah—are we stuck with developing some really strange, even unbiblical though popular, ways of thinking about God, ourselves, sin, and any possibility of hope. We've got to read on. Plots intend us to read on.

In truth, Jeremiah's leopard spots, Ethiopian skin, and sin with a diamond pen are all a setup—a huge one and a real one for sure but a setup nevertheless. It is a setup for Jeremiah's ultimate aha moment. It is a setup for the hint of resolution as Jeremiah points us toward the future. In a very similar way to Jeremiah's vivid depictions, the recurring reformations and revivals set us up to see the futility of simply "trying harder." This setup leads us, along with Jeremiah, to conclude, "We just can't do it! It's just who we are. It's written on our hearts. It is in our DNA, so to speak."

Just at the moment we believers are ready to conclude that somehow Jesus must be a cover-up for our own inability to love the Lord with all our heart, Jeremiah begins to speak a divine word about the ultimate intentions of the God plot: "The days are surely coming . . ." (Jer. 31:31). Without question, Jeremiah was clear and honest about the bleak reality of the human dilemma: leopard spots, Ethiopian skin, diamond pens. However, he is equally honest about the hope that God will ultimately deal with the human dilemma. Just listen to his words: "I will put my law [*torah*] *within* them, and I will write it on their hearts [*leb*]" (v. 33). Isn't it amazing? The very source of the dilemma to begin with, the *leb* ("heart"/"mind"/"will"/"decision-making processes"), will become the recipient of divine transformation. This God is just not satisfied with playing divine mind games and pretending everything in the covenant between him and his people is okay. He is determined and insistent that his people will ultimately carry out what he has called them to do: love him undividedly, with all their heart, all their soul, and all their strength.

Because the very will of God—the *torah* ("instruction"; one might go as far as to say the "mind of God")—is written upon the people's *leb* ("hearts"/"minds"), they will then authentically live out the covenant relationship God had intended from the start. No wonder Jeremiah concludes with what the result of this divine transformation of the *leb* will be: "I will be their God, and they shall be my people" (v. 33).

Much earlier, in the prophetic vision of Deuteronomy, we get a remarkable "hint" of the repeated prophetic call to turn back to God as well as Jeremiah's ultimate prophetic resolution. Just a slight change of words radically alters the original call in Deuteronomy 10:16 and the later call in 30:6. Echoes of the repeated prophetic call to *shub* ("turn"/"repent") are heard in 10:16: "Circumcise, then, the foreskin of your heart [*leb*], and do not be stubborn any longer." What a familiar prophetic call: change your ways, do something about your heart, and reform the way you think. But history tells us the real story. They can't; we can't! Listen now to the subtle but radical change that takes place in 30:6. Just as Jeremiah 31:31 describes the manner in which the covenant people who have been exiled to the ends of the world will return to the Promised Land, so, too, does Deuteronomy 30:1-5. Once the people have returned from their exile, verse 6 announces, "Moreover, the LORD your God will circumcise your heart [*leb*] and the heart [*leb*] of your descendants, so that you will love the LORD your God with all your heart and with all your soul, in order that you may live."

Isn't it amazing? Here we have been talking all this time about loving the Lord with undivided hearts/minds (*leb*), but we, like our ancestors, have sought resolution in our own feeble attempts to try harder, commit more, level one more holy hill, or burn one more idol. Then when we really get desperate, we dream up a resolution in which God will overcome our inability to change by playing divine mind games. We even have the audacity to call those mind games the love of God demonstrated through the faithfulness of Christ Jesus. But the resolution is right before our eyes in Deuteronomy 30:6. In order to love the Lord with all of our hearts and with all of our souls, the One who graced us first through deliverance, provision, and covenant must grace us again by circumcising, changing, our hearts/minds/wills— our *leb*. In order for us even to respond faithfully to the divine call to undivided love and untainted loyalty, God must change our very thought processes. Only then can we authentically love and genuinely trust this unique (holy) God without rival. Perhaps Elvina M. Hall had these same concerns and this same answer in mind when she wrote the memorable lyrics to the 1865 song "Jesus Paid It All":

> *Lord, now indeed I find,*
> *Thy pow'r, and Thine alone,*
> *Can change the leper's spots,*
> *And melt the heart of stone.*
> *Jesus paid it all;*
> *All to Him I owe;*
> *Sin had left a crimson stain;*
> *He washed it white as snow.*[1]

A Blessing

In the light of the prophetic call to wholeness and the ultimate prophetic resolution in the gracious, mind-transforming activity of God, Paul pronounces a blessing upon the church at Thessalonica that speaks hope into our fragmented fidelity. Look at the number of "wholeness" words italicized below, and look especially at Paul's conviction in bold concerning the way this blessing will ultimately come to fruition: "May the God of *peace* himself sanctify you *entirely*; and may your spirit and soul and body be kept *sound* [*complete*] and *blameless* at the coming of our Lord Jesus Christ. **The one who calls you is faithful, and he will do this**" (1 Thess. 5:23-24, emphasis added).

Reflecting on Our Place in the God Plot

In the God plot, God acts and calls, but what a dilemma we have in living out the call. But the God plot does not end with the dilemma. In fact, the God plot really intensifies with the dilemma. The primary Actor of this plot—God—is determined not to give up on his call. When he establishes covenant with his people—"I will be your God, and you will be my people" (Lev. 26:12, NLT)—he is serious about it. He is way too serious to let feeble human attempts at trying harder to be the end. He is far too committed to an authentic, reciprocal covenant relationship to play mind games with himself. If the dilemma is the heart (*leb*), then the same grace that delivered and provided for his people in the first place, the same grace that opened up a covenant relationship at the start—that grace will transform the source of the dilemma. That grace will actively engage in the heart itself "so that you will love the Lᴏʀᴅ your God with all your heart and with all your soul" (Deut. 30:6).

PART II

The God Plot—Priestly Style

As we now move to explore the way in which the priestly voice presents the God plot to us, we return to each of the primary elements of the God plot: setting, call, dilemma, and resolution. In some ways, having reached the hope for resolution in the prophetic voices of Jeremiah 31 and Deuteronomy 30, we actually could and maybe should jump ahead to the final major section (pt. 3) of this book and explore what that *leb* ("heart"/"mind") on which the *torah* ("instruction") of God is written looks like. However, the priestly voice is in direct dialogue with the prophetic voice on each movement of the God plot.

In some instances, the priestly voice simply restates or even duplicates what the prophetic voice has already articulated. Like the prophetic voice, the priestly voice grounds the God plot within the context or setting of divine grace as expressed through deliverance, provision, and covenant.

In other instances, however, the priestly voice actually enhances or even expands the prophetic voice. While the prophetic voice emphasizes "wholeness" of heart, or "complete" love, in relationship to the covenant God, the priestly voice uses its own vocabulary of "holiness," "cleanness," and "purity" to articulate this undivided loyalty. Seeing Yahweh God as uniquely distinct or different from the other gods of the ancient world, it calls him *holy*. Yet understanding the distinct relationship between the covenant people and their covenant God, it likewise calls upon the covenant people to be uniquely distinct or different from the surrounding nations, calling for them to be *holy* as well. The priestly voice particularly adds the uniquely ritual language of "uncleanness" to the plot of God as it attempts to describe the effect of infidelity upon the covenant people. Very closely related, the priestly voice adds the uniquely priestly language of "purity" or "pure heart" to describe the unadulterated devotion, untainted heart, in relationship to the Lord.

Yet in other instances, the priestly voice supplements the God plot with a whole other concern. This concern is perhaps one of the greatest contributions of the priestly voice to our understanding of the God plot and finding ourselves within it. This concern or supplement finds expression in the following questions: Why would the Lord have made a covenant with a community in the first place? How do the covenant people ultimately participate with God in his creative, redemptive task or mission in the world? It will help to keep these questions in mind, along with the other features of this overview, as we proceed with our look at Scripture's "other voice" as it articulates the God plot.

five

SETTING
PARTNERING WITH GOD
--GLORY BEARERS

FOR THE priestly voice, the setting in which the God plot occurs is the same as that for the prophetic voice. Like the prophetic voice, the priestly voice confesses and celebrates the three hinges of divine grace: deliverance, provision, and covenant. Having delivered the people from the hands of the Egyptians and having provided nourishment and protection in the wilderness, the Lord enters into a covenant with the people. In this covenant, he commits to a reciprocal relationship in which he will be their God and they will be his people.

As we have seen from the prophetic voice, the response of this unique covenant community was to be an undivided love, an unadulterated loyalty. The people whom the Lord had delivered and for whom he had provided were to be *wholly* his. Without rivals for their trust, they were to flesh out their fidelity to Yahweh in the daily affairs of life, from religion to politics to economics to everyday relationships.

While the priestly voice would understand this same reality of covenant fidelity, it takes the matter of covenant between God and his people a step further. The priests are particularly interested in the age-old question *why*. The priests are especially concerned with why God would call out a unique group of people to be a community in a unique covenant with him in the first place. Was it because he just had a special fondness for this group of people? Was it simply that he was a sovereign God and as such could redeem one group of people and damn another group at whim? Did this covenant have anything to do with their identity and role in the light of the rest of the world and all creation? Did it say something about their function in relationship to those who were not a part of the covenant community? In other words, why would God set this group of people apart to begin with?

A Kingdom of Priests

There is no more concise yet clear priestly statement that answers this question of *why* than one that appears right in the midst of the covenant ceremony between the Lord and his people in Exodus 19:4-6. Soon after the stories of divine deliverance from Egypt and divine provision of food in the wilderness, we read in chapter 19 that Moses went up onto Mount Sinai. There God spoke words to Moses, and in turn, Moses spoke those words to the people. From the priestly perspective, those words defined God's purpose for making a unique covenant with the people whom he had delivered. God says, "You have seen what I did to the Egyptians, and how I bore you on eagles' wings and brought you to myself. Now therefore, if you obey my voice and keep my covenant, you shall be my treasured possession out of all the peoples. Indeed, the whole earth is mine, but you shall be for me a priestly kingdom and a holy nation" (vv. 4-6).

Just as we saw in the prophetic voice, before covenant or obedience are ever mentioned in this key priestly passage, God's gracious activity appears first. Before God makes a covenant with the people, divine deliverance and provision take place. Any subsequent divine call to covenant fidelity is rooted in and emerges from the reality that God first acted graciously to save his people. The call to covenant keeping and obedience (*shema'*; see chap. 2 on the double meaning of "obey" and "hear") to the voice of God comes only after the divine deliverance and nourishment of the people.

As the graced people are faithful to the covenant with Yahweh, they will fulfill their function. The passage in Exodus 19 describes that role as a "treasured possession" (*segullah*). This treasured possession might best be understood as a portion of a larger whole that has been set apart from the larger whole. Most often when this unique word occurs in the Old Testament, it refers to God's covenant community that has been chosen by God to fulfill a unique role in the world. In Deuteronomy 7:6, 14:2, and 26:18, the people's role of being God's *segullah* is directly related to their being set apart (holy) by God from all other people groups. At first glance, this idea of being set apart would seem to indicate some type of special privileges. However, as God continues to speak in Exodus 19, he makes very clear, "Indeed, the whole earth is mine" (v. 5). In other words, every people group on the face of the earth is God's. He does not simply align himself with one group to save them and condemn the rest of the world. In fact, as we will soon discover in the remainder of the brief covenant passage, the only real reason God has a *segullah* is because all of the nations do belong to him. It will be the function of this "set apart portion" to carry out God's life-giving, delivering, providing, and covenant-making agenda for all nations.

Perhaps one of the most appropriate ways for us to understand the role of the covenant community in relationship to the rest of the world is through the double portion of inheritance an oldest son would receive in ancient Israel. If a family had four sons, the inheritance could be divided into five portions, with the oldest son receiving a double portion of the inheritance given to the other sons. However, this double portion was not given because the oldest son got "extra prizes" for being the parents' favorite. The double portion would indicate the oldest son's responsibility to the rest of the family. Particularly if and when the father died, the oldest son was to care for and provide for both the younger children and the mother. In the same way, the covenant community was God's *segullah*, God's set-apart, unique "treasured possession" that existed not for the sake of itself but for the sake of the family, the world. By no means was the covenant community somehow set apart as "God's favorite." Rather, it was the means of God's grace extended to the entire world.

So how did the priests describe this function of the covenant community? Interestingly, they used the language most familiar to them. They made reference to their own role in the community as priests to describe the role of the covenant people in relation to the world. According to the priestly voice, just as the priests were set apart in Israel to carry out their priestly mission, so also was the covenant community set apart in the world to carry out that same priestly mission. The covenant community was that unique group of people (i.e., a holy nation) set apart from the world, not to keep themselves separate from the world, but to step back into the world in order to function as priests to the world. They indeed were the "called out ones" (Gk., *ekklēsia*, "church") who were to function as a priestly community for the sake of the world.

So what was the role of the priests in Israel? Even more, what was the role of the priestly kingdom in the world? Among their different tasks, the priests would make sacrifices on behalf of the community. They would also determine what was life giving (clean) and what was life threatening (unclean) in the community. They would take what was unclean (threatening to life) and take steps to make it clean (encouraging to life), if at all possible.

Priests were particularly entrusted with providing the people with the instruction given by God. They taught and demonstrated the ways of God in the life of his people; they instructed the people in the will of God. Their duty was instruction (*torah*). They were to proclaim the faithful acts God had carried out in the life of his people and then to teach the people how to respond faithfully. When Exodus 19:4-6 reappears in 1 Peter 2:9, the church (the "called out ones" [*ekklēsia*]) is also described as "a chosen race, a royal priesthood, a holy nation, God's own people." It's no wonder that the writer of 1 Peter describes this priestly function as having to do with the instruction and proclamation of the ways of God: "in order that you may proclaim the mighty acts of him who called you out of darkness into his marvelous light" (v. 9).

Another extremely important—perhaps most important—role of the priests in the community is all too easily overlooked. Committed to God's primary agenda of life and the restoration of life, the priests were entrusted with the role of blessing the community. The most familiar priestly blessing upon the people of God that we have is found in Numbers 6:24-26: "The Lord bless you and keep you; the Lord make his face to shine upon you, and be gracious to you; the Lord lift up his countenance upon you, and give you peace."

What a remarkable task: pronouncing blessing upon the people. Numbers 6:27 refers to the task of blessing as putting God's name upon the covenant people. The priestly voice clearly seemed to understand that this most significant function of pronouncing blessing was now the task of the entire covenant community set apart (holy nation) to be a priestly kingdom. The community's mission was to place the name of God upon all people regardless of culture, language, creed, or ethnicity.

But what does it actually mean to *bless* the nations? The word "bless" is so nonchalantly thrown around as a cliché. From following up a sneeze to expressing an encouraging sentiment in a multitude of settings, "God bless you" has become an everyday phrase. But what does the word "bless" really mean? One of our greatest clues to its primary meaning is found in its first few appearances in the Bible. Repeatedly in Genesis 1, we read that God blessed his creation and said, "Be fruitful and multiply, and fill the earth" (e.g., v. 28). To bless is to speak life, fertility, hope, and a future into otherwise barren and hopeless people, situations, and places.

The priests had a bold and daring conviction. They dared to believe that while God was the Life Giver, they had a role in becoming a means or vessel of God's life-giving grace. They dared to imagine that while God was the Grace Bestower, they partnered with him as a dispenser or instrument of that grace. So what would it then look like for a community to see itself as a means of divine grace? Indeed, this community would be the human partner in the divine-human partnership. As they participated in the life of their covenant God, the covenant people would become the means of their God's grace and peace, mercy and love, to the world.

Blessed to Be a Blessing

What would this community of priestly blessing look like? The search for a portrait of that community takes us back to God's original call in Genesis 12 to a landless man and a barren woman who would eventually birth this covenant community. In his own standing, the nomad Abram could not produce land, for a nomad has no land to call his own. In her own standing, the barren Sarai could not produce children, for a barren woman has no capacity to do so. But into the infertility of both landlessness and barrenness, God makes a promise. He will *bless* this couple who cannot produce. Just as he blessed creation in Genesis 1 with life and fertility, he will *bless* them with signs of life, fertility, and hope. He will provide them land and descendants. However, he will not bless them simply for the sake of blessing them. This family is not blessed because somehow they are God's favorites. No, in fact, just as Exodus 19:4-6 has indicated, the whole earth belongs to God. All the nations, all the people groups, and all the cultures belong to him. But just as he uniquely calls a particular family to be set apart (i.e., a holy nation) in order to carry out the priestly responsibilities of life for the world, he calls that same community to be a blessing. They will become for the world the instruments of God's life-giving, hope-filled grace. They are not blessed for the sake of being blessed; they are blessed for the sake of becoming a blessing. They are participants with God in his mission on earth. A barren woman, a landless man, a group of slaves, wandering hungry nomads in the wilderness—all are blessed, delivered, and nourished to be a blessing, to deliver, and to nourish. They are given life to give life.

Glory Bearers

The priestly voice has one other unique way of describing what it means and looks like for the people of God to be set apart as a kingdom of priests. Much of the book of Exodus is concerned with describing in great detail just what it really entails to be this kingdom of priests. The second half of the book of Exodus is devoted to the priestly construction of the tabernacle. Soon after the covenant is concluded between God and his people, the Lord's instructions concerning the tabernacle begin in chapter 25 and continue until the end of the book. Only a brief interlude in chapters 32–34 interrupts the detailed description of the tabernacle. In chapters 25–31, instructions are given on how to build the tabernacle; in chapters 35–40, the people carry out the divine instructions as they actually construct the tabernacle. So what is the significance of these tabernacle instructions?

The answer to that question goes back to the verses just before the initial instructions about the tabernacle. In Exodus 24, Moses, Aaron, Aaron's two sons, and seventy elders of the community ascend Mount Sinai. At some point, Moses proceeds farther up onto the mountain. We then read these words in verses 15-17: "The cloud covered the mountain. The glory of the LORD settled on Mount Sinai, and the cloud covered it for six days; on the seventh day he called to Moses out of the cloud. Now the appearance of the glory of the LORD was like a devouring fire on the top of the mountain in the sight of the people of Israel."

The "glory of the LORD" becomes a dominant way the priestly voice talks about the presence of God among his people. So just what is this "glory of the LORD" that "settled" on the mountain and appeared as a "devouring fire"? The word in the biblical text that we now translate as "glory" is *kabod*. This word literally means "heavy." God's presence was so different from the ordinary life of the people that it was considered to be "weighty" or "heavy." This divine presence was so indescribably unique that to attempt a description was like looking directly into the bright sun in the middle of a sunny day. Therefore, this glory was depicted as bright, brilliant, blinding. It's no wonder that one of the most common ways of describing this brilliant and blinding otherness (glory) of God was as a bright light or a consuming fire. As Moses goes up the mountain into the presence of God, the story describes the radiant divine glory on the mountain. This God, together with his divine presence among his people, was completely other—that is, he was different from all else they had ever experienced.

Later when Israel became a nation, the priests had a remarkably creative way of demonstrating the blindingly bright otherness or weightiness of the divine glory. Every time they entered into the temple, they "saw" the demonstration of God's indescribable uniqueness. The windows of the temple were set near the ceiling in such a way that the sunlight would reflect off of the many objects and carvings with gold overlay. As the sun's rays reflected off the gold, the resulting light would be blinding to anyone entering the temple. The temple burst forth with the brilliant glory of the Lord. What a reminder of the heavy, weighty, bright otherness—the glory—of the God whose presence was represented in the temple in Jerusalem.

The narrative of God's covenant people would have proceeded without a hitch if this covenant God were like all of the other gods of the ancient world. But one unique characteristic set this God apart; it made him distinct (holy) from the other familiar deities. All the way from Syria's Baal to Greece's Zeus, gods ordinarily resided on mountains. A deity stayed on a mountain while the human devotees traveled to that mountain to worship that deity. However, the God with whom the people entered into covenant was different, very different. Perhaps it would be quite appropriate at this point for us to introduce the biblical word that has appeared already multiple times throughout this book. It is the word that ultimately means "different," "unique," or "separate": *holy*.

The very name of this covenant God, Yahweh, reflects just how different he was. The explanation of that name given to Moses in Exodus 3 demonstrates the uniqueness or *holiness* of his character. As described in verses 14-15, the name given to Moses emerges from the longer statement, "I will be whoever I will be" (see v. 14). While we often shorten the statement simply to "I am who/what I am" and then finally to "I am," the remainder of God's revelation to Moses in chapters 3–4 vividly clarifies an aspect of the unique (holy) character of this God. Yahweh points out that when

Moses goes to Pharaoh, God will be with Moses; when Moses goes to the people, God will be with Moses; and when Moses comes back to Mount Sinai, God will be with Moses. How unique for a God, how different, how *holy*! While gods ordinarily stayed back at their mountains and waited for their worshippers to return and worship them, this God traveled with his people. His very character demonstrated authentic covenant relationality. This covenant God was so committed to an authentic covenant relationship with his people that where they went, he was there with them. In fact, as a community they carried his presence into their journey; they bore his glory. No wonder in a subsequent conversation with God, Moses would boldly say, "If your presence will not go, do not carry us up from here. For how shall it be known that I have found favor in your sight, I and your people, unless you go with us? In this way, *we shall be distinct*, I and your people, from every people on the face of the earth" (33:15-16, emphasis added).

No wonder reassurances of God's presence are interwoven throughout Scripture. This relational presence demonstrates the very character, the unique (holy) character, of this covenant God. Consider just a few representative examples of this divine presence that are intricately interwoven into the very identity of the covenant people:

- To Abraham, "Do not be afraid, for I am with you and will bless you" (Gen. 26:24).
- To Jacob, "I am with you and will keep you wherever you go" (28:15).
- Concerning Joseph, "The Lord was with Joseph" (39:2).
- To Moses, "I will be with you" (Exod. 3:12).

- To Joshua, Moses said, "Be strong and courageous; do not be frightened or dismayed, for the Lord your God is with you wherever you go" (Josh. 1:9).
- To a generation in exile, "When you pass through the waters, I will be with you" (Isa. 43:2), and "I am with you . . . to save you" (Jer. 30:11).
- To Jeremiah, "Do not be afraid of them, for I am with you to deliver you" (1:8).
- To Jesus' disciples, "I am with you always" (Matt. 28:20).
- To Paul, "Do not be afraid, but speak and do not be silent; for I am with you" (Acts 18:9-10).

Relational presence with his covenant people is integral to the unique character of the Lord. In fact, this relational presence is integral to the plot of God as he calls into existence a covenant community.

Certainly all of these descriptions of the divine uniqueness sound wonderful: God goes with his people! But very soon, our ancestors at Mount Sinai recognized that they were going to have an overwhelming dilemma. God was not going to wait for them back at the mountain. Once they were ready to leave Sinai to journey through the wilderness to the Land of Promise, their covenant God in all of his uniqueness/glory would journey with them every step of the way. As the people prepared to set out with the completed tabernacle, the closing verses of Exodus sound very similar to those verses concerning the glory of God at Mount Sinai in Exodus 24:15-17: "Then the cloud covered the tent of meeting, and the glory of the Lord filled the tabernacle. . . . For the cloud of the Lord was on the tabernacle by day, and fire was in the cloud by night" (40:34, 38).

holiness

From the priestly perspective, the God plot thickens indeed. If the glory of God goes with his people, or better yet, if God doesn't stay back at Mount Sinai but sojourns with his people, then the covenant community functions as the *glory bearer* in the world. Isn't it amazing? This community *carries* the divine glory of God into the world. But how will that task occur? Between the description of the divine glory on Mount Sinai in 24:15-17 and that of the divine glory that travels with the people in 40:34-38, the priests construct a tabernacle for the divine presence, for the glory of God. This carefully constructed meeting place is not where the people meet each other but rather where God encounters Moses face-to-face. This tabernacle becomes the concrete image of the people's intertwined covenant relationship with their God. As they go into their world, their covenant God is with them. They bear his glory. Their presence in the world and his presence in the world are intricately related. To see the covenant people is to see the covenant God.

This intricate relationship between God and people really should not sound all that odd to us. The mutuality of the relationship between covenant God and covenant people is consistent throughout Scripture. As early as the opening creation story, humanity bears the image of God. For the early Christians, Paul describes the community we call the church as the "body of Christ." Corporately, the church embodies Jesus in the world; together, Christians *bear* Jesus Christ. They participate in the very life, death, and resurrection of their Messiah. The ultimate expression of this glory bearing is articulated magnificently in John's description of Jesus in John 1:14: "The Word became flesh and made his dwelling [tabernacle] among us. We have seen his *glory*, the *glory* of the one and only Son, who came from the Father, full of grace and truth" (NIV, emphasis added).

In the light of God's tabernacling presence with his glory-bearing people, it makes sense that the Lord would later adamantly reject David's idea of building him a temple. Because this covenant God was always "on the move" with his people, he refused to allow them to box him in. As we described earlier, he refused to be contained within any human construction (in other words, *an idol*). Do you recall God's response to David in 2 Samuel 7:6-7? "I have not dwelt in a house from the day I brought the Israelites up out of Egypt to this day. I have been moving from place to place with a tent as my dwelling. Wherever I have moved with all the Israelites, did I ever say to any of their rulers . . . , 'Why have you not built me a house of cedar?'" (NIV).

Under Solomon's leadership, the people eventually did construct God a house/temple. Even Solomon recognized that no humanly constructed temple could ever actually house the presence of this God. At the dedication of the temple, Solomon beautifully stated this reality in his prayer: "But will God indeed dwell on the earth? Even heaven and the highest heaven cannot contain you, much less this house that I have built!" (1 Kings 8:27).

Nevertheless, from generation to generation the temple came to be recognized by the covenant people as the Lord's residence. Even some of the psalms seem to understand the temple in this way:

How lovely is your dwelling place,
> O LORD of hosts!
My soul longs, indeed it faints
> for the courts of the LORD;

my heart and my flesh sing for joy
>   to the living God.
Even the sparrow finds a home,
>   and the swallow a nest for herself,
>   where she may lay her young,
at your altars, O Lord of hosts,
>   my King and my God.
Happy are those who live in your house,
>   ever singing your praise. (84:1-4)

I was glad when they said to me,
>   "Let us go to the house of the Lord!"
Our feet are standing
>   within your gates, O Jerusalem. (122:1-2)

But when all is said and done in the Christian narrative, God gets the final word! He had always planned that his divine presence would not be visited on a mountain or in a temple. Rather, his brightly shining glory would roam the earth through his covenant people. Paul describes the temple as follows: "Do you not know that you [plural] are God's temple and that God's Spirit dwells in you?" (1 Cor. 3:16). How amazing! In the end, the dwelling place of God continues to be with his people, on the move, roaming the world and never fossilized on a mountain or even in a permanent temple building. The covenant people of God continue to bear the glory, the tabernacling presence, of the Lord into the world. In their corporate body, they carry the unique otherness, the *holiness*, of their covenant God into the world with them. In the corporate body called the church, they carry the unique otherness, the *glory*, "of the one and only Son, who came from the Father, full of grace and truth" (John 1:14, NIV). The priestly vision is insistent that the glory will indeed tabernacle with the covenant people on the move. Why a covenant people? Because they are glory bearers!

But What Is This Glory?

We need to stay with this concept of God's glory for just a moment longer. It is easy for that word itself to become an overused cliché. In fact, the description above concerning glory could easily reinforce an almost cartoonlike perception of God's glory. It is all too easy to think of the divine glory as the green aura radiating from the Wizard of Oz as Dorothy and her three friends stand in his presence with fear and foreboding. The concept, however, is just too important in the priestly depiction of the God plot to stop short with the cartoon picture.

Do our scriptural ancestors provide us with any indication of what this *glory* of the Lord is really about? What is it about this God that is so blinding, so heavy, so other and different? Is there any other biblical depiction of this glory in addition to that of the heaviness and brightness of the Lord's otherness? What is this unique (holy) God really like? Can we discover anything about the divine character that sets this God (and consequently this covenant people) apart from anyone or anything else? Ultimately, what is it that the covenant people carry as they live, breathe, and journey in the world?

Tucked in between the intricate instruction of how to build the tabernacle in Exodus 25–31 and the detailed depiction of its actual construction in chapters 35–40, Moses makes a most provocative and bold statement to God. Moses first asks God, "How shall it be known that I have found favor in your sight, I and your people, unless you go with us? In this way, we shall be distinct, I and your people, from every people on the face of the earth" (33:15-16). He then proceeds to make this request: "Show me your glory, I pray" (v. 18).

In response to Moses' request, God is insistent that Moses will not be able see God's face. Moses will never be able to see God coming. He will never be able to predict or determine what the divine presence will look like in advance. However, he will be able to see his "back" (v. 23). He will indeed know that God has passed by, because all that is good, all that is life giving, about God will pass by Moses.

The moment of truth then arrives. Moses is about to discover just what this glory, this otherness, of God is all about. As the Lord descends and stands hidden within a cloud, the Lord proclaims in 34:6-7: "The LORD [Yahweh], the LORD [Yahweh], a God merciful and gracious, slow to anger, and abounding in steadfast love and faithfulness, keeping steadfast love for the thousandth generation, forgiving iniquity and transgression and sin."

From age to age, subsequent generations would return to this description concerning the incomparable otherness, the glory, of their covenant God. This defining statement that depicts the uniqueness (holiness) of God reappears at the most remarkable times: when the spies return with an alarming report about giants in the land (Num. 14:18); in Ezra's review of the Lord's faithfulness even in the midst of his people's infidelity (Neh. 9:17, 31); in a hymn of praise to God for his unique fidelity (Ps. 103:8); at the time of a great community fast during a locust plague (Joel 2:13); even when the archenemies, the Assyrians, repent and are delivered after the preaching of Jonah (Jon. 4:2). Like one of the ancient Christian confessions, this statement reminded subsequent generations of the covenant community of what set their covenant God apart from all other powers, both divine and human. What sets this God apart is his character of mercy, grace, slowness to anger, abounding steadfast love, faithfulness, and forgiveness.

If this statement paints a picture of the glory, uniqueness, and holiness of God, then what might the community that bears the divine glory look like? What does mercy, grace, slowness to anger, abounding steadfast love, faithfulness, and forgiveness look like as it is embodied in the glory-bearing community? How would a community that bears this glory appear in and engage with the world? Better yet, could we ever see this glory in flesh and blood so that we could observe what it looks like in real people?

According to the apostle John, we have indeed seen the fleshing out of the divine glory. The Word that was with God and was God has taken on flesh and blood (see John 1:1). Indeed, that glory has *tabernacled* among us in the same way that the divine glory filled the tabernacle in the wilderness. In Jesus Christ, we have seen the "*glory* of the one and only Son, who came from the Father, full of grace and truth" (v. 14, NIV, emphasis added). We truly have heard it with our ears, seen it with our eyes, and touched it with our hands (see 1 John 1:1).

What then would a community that dares to understand itself as the glory bearer, as the ongoing "fleshing out" of the glory of God, as the body of Jesus Christ, look like? Mercy, grace, slowness to anger, abounding steadfast love, faithfulness, forgiveness—all these descriptions somehow point forward to Paul's memorable hymn on faithful, selfless love: "Love is patient, love is kind. It does not envy, it does not boast, it is not proud. It does not dishonor others, it is not self-seeking, it is not easily angered, it keeps no record of wrongs. Love does not delight in evil but rejoices with the truth. It always protects, always trusts, always hopes, always perseveres. Love never fails" (1 Cor. 13:4-8, NIV).

Paul provides another amazing glimpse into that glory and the effects of it upon the glory-bearing community as he paints a picture of the mind of Christ in Philippians 2:3-4: "Do nothing from selfish ambition or conceit, but in humility regard others as better than yourselves. Let each of you look not to your own interests, but to the interests of others."

Covenant Connected to Mission: The Mission of God and His People

The priestly vision understands a direct correlation between the covenant of God and his people and the purpose or mission of the covenant community. Even more, the mission of God's people is directly related to the mission of God in the world: they are a kingdom of priests and a holy nation, blessed to be a blessing, and tabernacle-building glory bearers. The mission of the covenant people is caught up in the mission of their covenant God. The priestly voice would certainly conclude that this covenant community is set apart *from* the nations to live *in and among* the nations so that it can be the instrument of divine blessing and grace *to* the nations. The covenant people's separation (holiness) from the world is for their engagement with the world and their life in it. Priestly people, like God, seek the agenda of life. They seek it because they themselves are to be a blessing and because as glory bearers they are the embodiment—the incarnation—of the glory of God.

six

CALL
HOLY GOD, HOLY PEOPLE

THE PRIESTLY VISION was boldly and unabashedly convinced that the community in covenant with God spoke the priestly blessing of life into the world; it was the bearer of God's glory in the world. As the Lord was merciful, gracious, slow to anger, abounding in steadfast love, faithful, and forgiving, so also was the covenant community in its relationships with others. The tabernacling presence of God journeyed with his people in their world; as they went, God was with them. The priestly vision firmly believed that the God who had delivered and provided for the covenant community had in turn entered into a covenant relationship with it, not for its own sake, but for the sake of all nations and ultimately for the sake of all creation. The phrase "covenant for the sake of the world" perhaps best summarizes the priestly context of the God plot.

In the context of "covenant for the sake of the world," the priestly vision makes a unique call upon the life of the covenant community. This call is directly linked to what also becomes the primary priestly question: how can a community comprised of human beings ever authentically participate in the life-giving blessing, purpose, and mission of God? Stated in a more priestly fashion: how can a community of common humans ever bear the glory of an uncommon God? The priestly story of the human race demonstrates humanity's consistent penchant for self-serving power and life-taking violence. Only a few chapters into the scriptural narrative, God himself concludes that every inclination of the human heart/mind (*leb*) is evil continually. He makes this conclusion not only before the great flood (Gen. 6:5) but also following it (8:21).

The priestly vision understood that humanity leans into all that is contrary to the God who is merciful, gracious, slow to anger, abounding in steadfast love, faithful, and forgiving. Yet this unique (holy) God has entered into a partnership, a covenant, with a community of human beings. How ironic! Humans who are inclined to self-serving power and life-taking violence are now participants in the plot of a God who uses divine power for the sake of the other and who is committed to life-giving deliverance and provision. Talk about polar opposites: self-serving power called to reflect self-giving power? Life-taking violence called to life-giving deliverance and provision? Is this a cruel divine joke? Is it the riddle of the ultimate divine-human oxymoron? How can a human community bent on violence and self-serving power ever even begin to reflect what makes this God so different? How can it bear his glory? How can it image his holiness?

Into this context, the priestly vision issues succinctly but ever so poignantly a divine call to the covenant community: "Be holy, because I the LORD your God am holy" (see Lev. 11:44-45; 19:2; 20:7; see also the New Testament repetition of this call in 1 Pet. 1:13-16). This call is to the priestly vision what the call to love the Lord with all the heart, soul, and strength is to the prophetic vision.

As we mentioned earlier in our discussion about clichés and code words, people of faith seem to throw the words "holy" and "holiness" around all the time. These words permeate our ancient hymns and contemporary praise songs. They linger on our lips as we pray. They appear and reappear in our sermons. They echo in our Bible study conversations. Across the diverse traditions of the Christian faith, we unanimously agree that the call of God to his people is to be holy. No one anywhere can get away from the reality of this divine call to the covenant community. But what is this call about?

The notion of holiness ("holy," "sanctify," "sanctification"—it is all from the same root word in the Old Testament language) brings so many preconceived ideas with it. Because of these preconceived ideas, it is of great value first to reflect briefly on what our own notions may be. Sometimes we have a preconceived image of "holy people" as those who carry out certain pious actions. They pray consistently, read the Scriptures devoutly, and attend church regularly. Sometimes the preconceived image is just the opposite. Rather than engaging in certain pious activities, "holy people" refrain from specific evil activities. They refuse to go to certain places, say certain things, or carry out certain actions. Other times, the preconceived notion is that "holy people" either wear or avoid wearing certain kinds of clothing or ornaments. We may also imagine "holy people" to be those who stand aloof or apart from the world, society, and culture in which they live. At other times, we may have the preconceived notion that we become "holy people" by praying a certain kind of prayer of dedication. Perhaps we are even given a formulaic prayer to pray to "make us holy."

Beyond the many preconceived notions we may bring to the language of holiness, perhaps one of the greatest struggles with the language emerges from the double use of the language in Scripture, prayer, hymnody, and sermons. God himself is holy, but we are called to be holy. Isn't that exactly what the priestly call says? "Be holy, because I the LORD your God am holy." Bringing certain preconceived ideas of the holiness of God into this call, we may become so bewildered that we conclude that if humans are called to be like God, then this call must be no more than a hopeless ideal. As a result, we can very quickly and easily dilute or even dismiss the call. In the frantic, misunderstood attempt to be like God, we may tend to set abnormal, even unhealthy, standards that can never quite be attained. Thus we can quickly become discouraged, distraught, defeated, and even paralyzed.

"Be holy, because I the LORD your God am holy." What in the world does this call mean? This call just cannot— must not—be divorced from and lifted out of the God plot to stand on its own. To take the call to be holy out of the priestly covenant context is to limit the call to such things as pious actions, outward appearance, aloofness or exclusivity, and specific prayers or rituals of sanctification. These then become ends in themselves—that is, piety for the sake of piety, appearance for the sake of appearance, exclusivity for the sake of exclusivity, and so on.

Rather than being meant to stand on its own, this call is specifically set within the covenant between God and his people. Notice the phrase "I the LORD [Yahweh] your God." This line is central to the call, since it assumes the covenant between Yahweh and his people: "I will be *your God*, and you will be my people" (Lev. 26:12, NLT, emphasis added). As we have seen, the priestly perspective is insistent that the Lord's covenant people fulfill the unique task of bearing the glory of their covenant God into the world. As they journey, they carry the uniqueness of their delivering and providing covenant God. They demonstrate a clear "family resemblance" to their covenant God. They bear his unique character of mercy, grace, slowness to anger, abounding steadfast love, faithfulness, and forgiveness.

Their unique covenant God stands in direct and sharp contrast to the powers that enslave and to the principalities that take. This divine power, however, is different or *holy*. Rather than enslaving and oppressing, he delivers. Rather than taking or hoarding, he provides. Rather than unilaterally micromanaging, he bilaterally covenants. Even though it means taking a risk, he dares to partner. Deliverer, Provider, covenant Partner—how different, unique—*holy*!

And now this covenant community has become the other end of the covenant partnership. They now become participants in deliverance, provision, and covenant fidelity with their neighbor, even with their enemies. Indeed, they have been given life (blessed) so that they might become instruments of life giving (a blessing). As a covenant people, they bear the tabernacling presence of God into the world. The priestly voice operates on the conviction that this delivered, nourished, and covenanted people now join their unique (holy) covenant God on a unique (holy) mission as a unique (holy) people in the world.

The call to be holy because God is holy is in direct relationship to a people who have joined God on the divine mission. The call is in direct correlation to what it means to be a community *set apart* (i.e., "holy nation" in Exod. 19:6) in order to be priests to the world. It is directly linked to the tabernacling presence of God that refuses to reside on a mountain but insists on being fleshed out in the glory-bearing community. From the priestly perspective, the covenant community becomes the incarnation of this unique (holy) God. As he was utterly unique or set apart (holy) from all other powers, both divine and human, they, too, must be utterly unique (holy) if they are to embody him appropriately.

Holy God? Holy People?

Certainly this God of the covenant community is different from all human beings. He is God; humans are human. But for the priestly vision, this covenant God is different from all the other gods as well. How? When we stop short with the explanation that God is holy, the difference or the holiness of God becomes the character trait of God in and of itself. We stop without ever asking, "How is this God different? How is he unique? How is he holy?" As a result, we are left with the long-held and highly esteemed interpretation of what some might call the *mysterium tremendum*, the "great mystery."[1] God is simply other. Nothing else is comparable. He is the Great Mystery.

What a true statement! However, the God plot is not satisfied simply to say that God is different for the sake of being different. It refuses simply to stop short with divine *uniqueness* or *holiness* as the character trait. It is deeply interested in how this God is unique. As the God plot unfolds in Scripture, it is insistent that the Great Mystery, the Holy One, has made known his difference to us. This statement is certainly not to deny the awesome and beautiful mystery that remains of God. We could never fully explain this God. However, the covenant people dared to believe that they had caught glimpses of what it is that makes this God so different, so unique, so holy. The nature of God's uniqueness or holiness has been demonstrated through divine act after divine act. And as if these life-giving, delivering, providing, and covenant-making acts were not enough, it has ultimately been demonstrated in flesh and blood through Jesus Christ.

From the outset, the otherness of this God began to be expressed through the narrative of a divine Creator who makes room for that which is other than himself. Wherever there might be the threat to life, he divides—just as he later will divide the waters at the Red Sea. Dividing darkness with light, and chaotic waters with a firmament, he makes room for life to thrive. Refusing to act as a micromanager, this God who is different releases any form of unilateral, self-serving power and proceeds to empower his creatures to participate in his ongoing creative activity. He entrusts tasks to his creatures and partners with them. The light divides; the firmament separates; the land holds back the sea; the earth sends forth plants and animals; the sun and the moon rule; the waters swarm with sea creatures; and the humans rule, domesticate, serve, and watch over. To all living creatures, he then grants the capacity to continue and propagate life: "Be fruitful . . . multiply . . . fill" (e.g., Gen. 1:22).

In himself relational ("Let us make . . ." [v. 26]), this unique God forms creative masterpieces that reflect his relational character. Shaping different realities of relationality, he creates relationship between himself and his creation, relationship between himself and the human race, relationship between his creation and the human race, relationship among the creatures, and relationship among human beings. His creation becomes an intricate web of interrelationality.

Are you beginning to get the picture? This Deity is not greedy for power, nor is he a micromanaging manipulator. In the opening chapters of the divine story, we see vivid and definitive demonstrations of self-emptying power in its purest forms. This God is indeed different from all we have ever known of divine or human power, gods or kings. From the outset, he is *holy*—unique—in his self-emptying use of power and in his life-giving use of creativity.

The otherness of this unique (holy) God becomes even clearer as the God plot unfolds beyond creation. This God was so deeply committed to what he had created that when it became marred in his hands, he did not utterly destroy it. Instead, he invited Noah and his family to participate with him in his ongoing creative work. He simply would not permit infidelity, violence, and self-serving power to be the final nail in the coffin of his creative work.

And the difference (holiness) of this God continued as he made a promise to barren and landless people, as he rescued slaves from oppression and guided them safely through a threatening wilderness. Never giving up on his divine promise and commitment to his covenant people, he repeatedly partnered with human messengers (prophets). These messengers spoke words of warning and repentance and of hope and restoration to the covenant community, all the while yearning for the people to finally hear the word of the Lord. Even when the people lost their religious and political props through exile, God entered the exile with them. Through these mighty acts and more, God demonstrated his difference and uniqueness quite vividly.

Finally Christian Scripture takes us to the pinnacle of this God's difference or holiness. Vulnerably, he wrapped himself up in flesh and blood and pitched his tent among us. Refusing to exercise self-serving power, he demonstrated his love—his never-ending fidelity and commitment—to his followers by becoming a servant and washing their feet. He then demonstrated his never-dying commitment to the world by giving his very life for the world. He continued to be the vulnerable, partnering God by calling disciples to follow him and a church to incarnate him. He continued his self-emptying partnership with his church by sending his Holy Spirit so that his followers would not be left alone to carry out the mission of God.

Clearly, the difference or holiness of this covenant God was not in his pious actions, in his clothes and hairstyle, in his withdrawal from the world, or in a prayer that he prayed. Far too often the people of God both before and after Jesus Christ have legitimated many of their oddities or unique idiosyncrasies by reasoning that because God stands out (is holy), then they, too, should invent unique oddities that will cause them to stand out. Now don't misunderstand what we are saying; the people of God from generation to generation should find ways to stand out from the powers and principalities that dominate their society and culture. But the people of God are absolutely not called to be peculiar for the sake of being peculiar. The call to be holy is not for the sake of oddity or uniqueness in and of itself.

God has already shown us what makes him different. Through his actions and ultimately through his own incarnation, he has revealed to us what makes him holy. The uniqueness of this God is demonstrated in his life-giving use of divine power to deliver the enslaved, to provide for the needy, and to remain faithful to the covenant he has made. His glory is not simply a celebration of the atypical and the unconventional. His glory is what no other powers, whether divine or human, are known for: mercy, grace, slowness to anger, abounding steadfast love, faithfulness, and forgiveness. What sets this God apart and what will set his people apart is wonderfully expressed in the first epistle of the apostle John:

> Beloved, let us love one another, because love is from God; everyone who loves is born of God and knows God. Whoever does not love does not know God, for God is love. . . .
>
> Beloved, since God loved us so much, we also ought to love one another. No one has ever seen God; if we love one another, God lives in us, and his love is perfected in us. . . .
>
> God is love, and those who abide in love abide in God, and God abides in them. (1 John 4:7-8, 11-12, 16)

We may create all of the "oddities" we desire and most certainly can call them holiness. Indeed, they would be just that; they would be uniquely other, oddly different. However, we have seen firsthand what sets this God of covenant apart from all other powers, both human and divine—self-giving, self-emptying love that moves beyond sentimental feeling and acts for the sake of deliverance, provision, and covenant.

Within the priestly vision, the language of holiness/holy or sanctification/sanctify is not nearly as complicated as we have sometimes tried to make it. The language is directly related to what we have been describing in previous chapters—the uniqueness of God. From the priestly perspective, this covenant God was indeed different from all other powers. The covenant people were set apart (holy nation) to partner with their covenant God on his creative mission of life-giving blessing. Like their covenant God, they were different in how they would use their power or capacity to act in the lives of others. Rather than living by the survival tactics of oppression, destruction, hoarding, and so on, they would embody the difference (holiness) of their God by living and by giving up their lives for the sake of life, blessing, deliverance, provision, and faithfulness. When asked which commandment was the greatest, Jesus summarized concisely and clearly this uniqueness of living and dying for the sake of the other: "'You shall *love* the Lord your God with all your heart, and with all your soul, and with all your mind.' This is the greatest and first commandment. And a second is like it: 'You shall *love* your neighbor as yourself.' On these two commandments hang all the law and the prophets." (Matt. 22:37-40, emphasis added).

seven

DILEMMA
IDOLATRY, IMPURITY,
AND ICHABOD

"BE HOLY, because I the LORD your God am holy." Uh-oh! Within the priestly perspective, the covenant people really have a problem now. How in the world can this group of people called to be set apart as the glory bearers in the world even begin to carry out their task? How can the commonplace—the unholy—ever think about bearing the tabernacling presence of this holy God into the world?

The essential dilemma we have seen in the prophetic voice is at the heart of the dilemma in the priestly voice as well: sacred cows, holy hills, and substitute kings and alliances (see discussion in chap. 3). Since divine images were most often associated with the holy sites (temples) where priests would carry out their daily tasks, it makes sense that the priestly voice would express the mind-set and practices of sacred cows, holy hills, and substitute kings and alliances in a single word: "idolatry."

In the book of Exodus, a defining moment in the life of the covenant people is located between the instructions for building the tabernacle (chaps. 24–31) and its actual construction (chaps. 35–40). As they become impatient with Moses, they participate in what will become their perennial problem. They shape an idol. Actually, their priest Aaron leads the way!

From the priestly perspective, the God plot intensifies with the covenant people's engagement in idolatry. If the mission of this unique covenant God in the world is intricately linked to the covenant community, it now appears to be impossible for this unfaithful covenant community to adequately bear the glory of God in the world. Their lives would be double-talk, even falsehood. How can they be the unique glory bearers of Yahweh in the world when internally as a community they are climbing the holy hills, building the sacred cows, and looking to other kings and alliances to fight their battles? How can they bear the uniqueness of their God if they themselves turn their loyalty to alternative political, economic, and religious systems? Better yet, can there even be a covenant people if they have broken covenant?

In the sacred cow narrative of Exodus 32–34, God's first response to this question is, "Absolutely not!" As a result of the Lord's initial response, he begins to negotiate with Moses, promising Moses that he will make a covenant with him alone. However, he will let the people go their own way. Although Moses carries on an engaging and convincing argument with God, once Moses actually hears and sees for himself what the people have done, he reacts just as God did: "Absolutely not! This covenant cannot continue!" Shattering the tablets of the covenant (i.e., breaking the covenant), Moses sees no way out for the people. Honestly, Moses and God both seem to have it right. It just doesn't make sense that a community of infidelity could give witness to the world concerning a God of fidelity. It's an oxymoron; to use the old cliché, "It is like mixing oil and water." It is impossible, so it seems, for the covenant people to authentically be the glory bearers.

The matter of the incapacity of the people of God to bear the glory of God reaches a climactic crescendo centuries later during the prophetic ministry of Ezekiel. Although Ezekiel was called to be a prophet later in life, he was most intimately familiar with the priestly perspective, language, and images. He had carried out the priestly tasks in the Jerusalem temple before the exile and had been carried away into Babylonian exile with his fellow priests.

Known for his imaginative and often bizarre ways of speaking, Ezekiel recounts a graphic vision in Ezekiel 8. It is the vision of a tour through the temple in Jerusalem. By this time in the story of God's people, the temple had replaced the tabernacle. The once mobile tabernacle that bore the glory of God as the people traveled through the wilderness had become a permanent fixture that many thought "contained" the glory of God. As Ezekiel tours through this glory-bearing temple, he sees indescribable atrocities taking place. Each atrocity is associated with the infidelity of the people as they engage in all sorts of practices that offer the same fertility, life, and hope as that offered by holy hills, sacred cows, and substitute kings.

Even before going into the temple, Ezekiel sees the "idol of jealousy" (v. 5, NIV), likely an image of the fertility goddess Asherah. The Lord warns Ezekiel before going into the temple that what he is preparing to see are "great abominations" (v. 6) that will ultimately drive God's glory far away from the temple itself.

As Ezekiel makes his way into the temple, he sees odd drawings of unclean animals on the wall. From the priestly perspective, these unclean animals were indications that life-taking rather than life-giving practices were being carried out not only in the city but also in the glory-bearing temple itself. Alongside these drawings were various idols, human creations that attempted to encapsulate and manipulate divine power. Ezekiel sees as many as seventy of the community's leaders as they stand in a posture of worship before the drawings of life-taking destruction and before the images of encapsulated and manipulated divine power. Each leader burns incense in devotement to the representations. Moreover, not only are the leaders corporately carrying out these acts of worship, but each one also has his own shrine room with his own personal idol. Simply for the sake of survival, every attempt to construct an idol and lean toward life-taking destruction has found a safe place in the glory-bearing temple.

As Ezekiel's temple tour continues, he comes to the north gate of the temple. There he sees a group of women seated on the ground. They are carrying out the rites of lamentation and grief for the fertility god Tammuz. When the summer heat had beat down upon the crops and destroyed them, the popular god Tammuz was understood to have died. Therefore, the worshipping women grieve his death in hopes that he will resurrect and bring fertility, life, and hope back to the land. In the precincts of the glory-bearing temple, the survival tactic of Tammuz has found its home.

purity

Ezekiel's final stop in his temple tour is perhaps the apex of the atrocities of uncleanness. In the very spot where priests station themselves to pray to their covenant God now stands twenty-five men who face toward the east, their backs to the temple. They are lying prostrate in front of the sun. How remarkable! With their backs to the Lord, they pay homage and honor to the god of the empire, Shemesh. In order to survive the great atrocities of war and destruction, the covenant people make a home for the popular god of the empire.

It would seem that all of these acts of infidelity and life-taking uncleanness in the glory-bearing temple are atrocious enough. However, the Lord indicates to Ezekiel that outside of the temple, the covenant community actively engages in acts of violence (*hamas*) against the weak of the community. Life taking, destruction, and death are everywhere.

Impurity

How can the glory bearers, the instruments of divine blessing, the covenant people participating in a life-giving divine mission embody these tasks when the glory-bearing temple is filled with life-taking idols? In hearing this question, we cannot help but again hear, as we did in chapter 5, Paul ask the church, "Do you not know that you [plural] are God's temple and that God's Spirit dwells in you?" (1 Cor. 3:16). How can the unique (holy) divine presence that distinguishes the covenant community continue to dwell in the midst of a violent, life-taking community? How can a holy God inhabit an unholy people?

The priests had a unique way of describing the contamination brought about by the people's resorting to sacred cows and holy hills. They developed their own language, which was grounded in their understanding that all of life was divided into what gives life and what takes life. Whatever was life giving or life enhancing, they named *clean* or *pure*. Whatever was life taking or life destroying, they named *unclean* or *impure*.

From the priestly perspective, what Ezekiel saw both in the temple and outside of the temple was unclean. It was impure. It threatened life. It was deathly. In Ezekiel 36:25, the prophet specifically associates idolatrous practices with the uncleanness of the people. As they participated in the idolatry of holy hills and sacred cows in the temple and in the violence outside of the temple, they had become life takers rather than life givers. The people called by God to join in God's mission of blessing had engaged in just the opposite of blessing; they had involved themselves in a destructive, life-taking curse.

Often we tend to associate the biblical language of uncleanness or impurity with some type of filthy spiritual substance residing within us. We may call that spiritual substance *Sin with a capital S* or *inbred sin*. We tend to conclude that if somehow we can just get that substance out of us, then everything will be fixed. We then associate *cleansing* or *purification* with the removal of that filthy substance.

But from Ezekiel's perspective, the uncleanness was not a mere substance that needed to be taken out or extracted from the people. For Ezekiel, and ultimately for the priestly vision, the issue was much deeper. The issue centered on a covenant that had gone terribly wrong on the part of the covenant community. Call it what you will—infidelity, unfaithfulness, disloyalty—the relationship of the covenant community to their covenant God was the furthest thing from faithful. From the priestly vantage point, the idolatrous and violent practices had made the covenant people as unclean as one who secretes bodily fluids such as blood or semen. Like bodily fluids, these practices of idolatry within the temple of God and the violence outside it threatened to contaminate the entire life of the community.

So let's return to our previous question. How can the glory-bearing community ever begin to carry out the task of embodying the divine glory in the world when it stands in sharp contrast to the God whose glory it is to bear? How can a life-taking community continue to bear witness to a life-giving God? How can a God who is so different (holy) in his life-extending love inhabit a community that is anything but different (unholy) in their life-taking worship and violence? It just cannot continue! They just cannot carry the glory—"Ichabod!"

Ichabod

Ezekiel's response to the covenant community's failure to faithfully carry out its task of glory bearing can best be described as *Ichabod*. We know this term from that fascinating story in 1 Samuel 4 in which the Philistines capture the ark of the covenant. On hearing the news that the ark was captured and that his sons were dead, Eli fell backward, broke his neck, and died. Then on hearing of the deathly events that had taken place, Eli's pregnant daughter-in-law gave birth to a son and named him Ichabod, meaning "No Glory!" As she named him, she announced, "The glory has departed from Israel" (v. 22).

The narrative of Ichabod only begins to paint the reality that Ezekiel is about to describe concerning the temple. The priestly prophet clearly understands that the glory of God cannot continue to stay with the glory bearers. The glory-bearing community has refused to faithfully carry out its co-mission from God. It has become adulterated with and contaminated by all that is in direct contrast to the life-giving, delivering, faithful God. As the covenant community (the temple) now bears the image of destruction, oppression, violence, and infidelity, Ezekiel proceeds to depict the manner in which the glory, the *kabod*, must rise from the temple and depart. Indeed, this is *'i-kabod*, "no more glory."

Ezekiel's vision of the departure of the glory of God is not the depiction of some type of divine temper tantrum. It is simply the reality of the situation. When the temple of the Lord (i.e., the covenant community) stands in such sharp contrast to all that this unique (holy) God is, it simply is not bearing the glory! How can infidelity and disloyalty give witness to the God of fidelity and faithfulness? How can violence give witness to the God of life and creation? To use the familiar cliché, "The round peg cannot fit into the square hole." The life takers do not reflect the Life Giver. Infidelity does not reflect fidelity. Undoubtedly the glory—what makes this God unique—just doesn't dwell in the temple!

eight
RESOLUTION
PREPARED FOR THE GLORY

SO IS THERE any hope? Is there any resolution? If the people of God are so determined to continue to climb holy hills and build sacred cows, can they ever fulfill their task of being the divine glory bearers to the world? If the very glory that they are to carry into the world departs, is the God plot over? Has the divine call upon God's covenant community to be a kingdom of priests, a holy nation, a blessing to and for the sake of the world, come to an abrupt end?

We have seen the way the prophetic voice at first understood the resolution to the human dilemma to be in the humanly initiated activities of reform and attempts to return to God. In the same way, the priestly voice understood the resolution to the dilemma to be in specific priestly activities or rituals of purification. The priests articulated the aftereffects of all that is antithetical to God and particularly to God's agenda of life as uncleanness or impurity. So the resolution must somehow be related to the priestly task of making the unclean clean, the impure pure.

The roots of cleansing or purification rituals go far back in human history. These types of rituals are certainly not unique to the priests found within the pages of Scripture. To go into extensive discussion of the various rites of purification or cleansing could tend to take us too far away from our primary concern here. However, in order to understand the initial response of the priestly voice to the human dilemma of mistrust in and lack of fidelity toward God, we must gain at least a glimpse into what the priests thought concerning purification or cleansing.

It probably comes as little surprise to even the most casual reader of the Bible that the book that goes into the most explicit details of the cleansing ritual is the "priestly handbook" known as Leviticus. However, the book of Numbers is also very concerned about addressing issues of cleanness and uncleanness, purity and impurity. The priests gave significant attention to categorizing animals, foods, and actions that would make a person unclean.

From the priestly perspective, what one might call ritual impurity was understood to be the result of various natural, often necessary, activities of the human body. These activities included contact with a corpse, skin diseases (often regarded as leprosy), and the discharges of bodily fluids such as semen and blood. Just as contagious diseases are viewed today, the impurity from these bodily fluids was also understood to be contagious from one person to another.

From the priestly perspective, what one might call moral impurity was understood to be the result of transgressing specific divine stipulations, such as those forbidding murder, various sexual acts, and corruptions in worship. Among all of the transgressions understood to engender moral impurity, however, idolatry stood at the forefront within the priestly vision. The priests were convinced that the practice of idolatry and the worship of deities other than the Lord not only made the individual unclean but especially made the temple of the Lord and the Lord's Holy Land unclean (e.g., Lev. 18:28; 20:3; Jer. 32:34; Ezek. 5:11; 23:38-39). Because of the contagious character of uncleanness or impurity, the effect of uncleanness upon the land and the temple was especially a concern for the priests. Thus any member of the community who was understood to have become unclean and yet who did not participate in the priestly rituals of cleansing was eventually cut off from the community. From the priestly perspective, that person had made the earthly "dwelling places" of the Lord—the temple and the Land of Promise—unclean (see Num. 19:20).

The Priestly Vision in the Prophetic Ezekiel

In the attempt to depict the dilemma of the people of God to trust the Lord undividedly and the effects of that dilemma within the unfolding plot of God, Ezekiel provides the most articulate priestly presentation in Scripture. No voice in the Bible gives us clearer insight into the priestly understanding of the uncleanness brought about by covenant infidelity and the attempted resolution found in the ritual of cleansing.

While Ezekiel is certainly found among the prophets of ancient Israel, he is unique among them. As we mentioned earlier, although he carries out a prophetic ministry during the time of exile, before he was deported into Babylonian exile along with many of the leaders of Jerusalem, he was a priest in the Jerusalem temple. As a result of his background as a priest, his prophetic messages are filled with priestly language, ideas, and convictions.

In the previous chapter, we saw how Ezekiel describes the practices of idolatry and the worship of other gods in the Jerusalem temple (Ezek. 8). In a subsequent oracle, he announces to Jerusalem: "A city! Shedding blood within itself; its time has come; making its idols, defiling itself. You have become guilty by the blood that you have shed, and defiled by the idols that you have made" (22:3-4). We noted the way Ezekiel demonstrates the priestly conviction that this God who is so unique, so different, so holy, cannot continue to abide with or be worshipped in a temple that has become so unclean with idols; the tabernacling otherness or glory of the Lord that the people were to bear in the world must depart from the unclean temple. God's temple has become a location of death (i.e., uncleanness) rather than a location of life (i.e., cleanness). Moreover, as Ezekiel continues, he indicates that God's Holy Land has also become unclean; it, too, is a location of death. Because the covenant people have made the land of the Lord unclean through their practices of idolatry, covenant infidelity to the Lord, and violence to their neighbor, they also must now depart God's unique (holy) land. They will be exiled from the land. To use the priestly language of Leviticus 18:25, 28, the land will now "vomit out" the people who have made the land unclean (i.e., deathly rather than life giving).

A Glimpse of Resolution

Having depicted the effect of the human dilemma upon the people of God through describing the departure of the divine glory from the temple, Ezekiel, or perhaps we should say God himself, refuses to let "Ichabod" be the final word of the God plot! For Ezekiel, the glory departs only so God's people, temple, and land might be prepared to faithfully bear the glory when it returns. The God plot continues, and once again its focus is on what God will graciously do in the life of his covenant people who have struggled from generation to generation with holy hills, sacred cows, and substitute kings.

This God is absolutely determined that his temple, his covenant people, his glory bearers, will indeed fulfill their task of bearing his name to the world. They will indeed carry out the mission given to their father Abraham and their mother Sarah to be blessed by God so that they might be instruments of divine blessing to all the nations.

Ultimately this covenant people who have been separated or "called out" (Gk., *ekklēsia*, "church") to be the kingdom of priests in the world are so interconnected with their covenant God that the lives they live directly reflect or "image" (see Gen. 1:27) God himself. Thus God announces in Ezekiel 36:22: "It is not for your sake, O house of Israel, that I am about to act, but for the sake of my holy name, which you have profaned among the nations to which you came." Again in verse 32, the Lord repeats, "It is not for your sake that I will act, says the Lord GOD." What God is about to do in the life of his covenant people is directly tied to their purpose or mission as the glory bearers, as the image of God, as the means of divine blessing to the world. They are so intricately tied to the Lord himself that God will now act for the sake of his own reputation. And what will he do? Ezekiel makes the grand announcement of the divine resolution to the human dilemma: "I will sanctify my great name . . . when through you I display my holiness before their eyes" (v. 23).

Because the English translation often uses two distinct English words ("sanctify" and "holiness"), we don't quite get the real sense of what the biblical text is saying. The two words are actually from the same root word, *qadash* ("to make holy," i.e., "to sanctify"). Literally, the divine resolution for the glory bearers who have all too often done everything but bear the divine uniqueness to the world is, "I will set my name apart [i.e., "sanctify"] . . . when I set you apart [i.e., "sanctify"] in front of the nations."

Amazing! How much more intricately related can a covenant God and a covenant people be? As this God sets his people apart (for the sake of glory bearing not simply for the sake of being set apart), he will set his own reputation apart. The sanctifying act of God in the life of his people is all for the sake of the reputation/name of God! To the glory of God! No wonder the Westminster Shorter Catechism, completed in 1647, contained this first question and response: "What is the chief end of man? Man's chief end is to glorify God, and to enjoy him forever."[1] Glory bearers made in the divine image, blessed to be a blessing—this covenant God is so determined that the people to whom he has committed himself will bear his name and reputation appropriately that he himself will act "not for your sake, . . . but for the sake of my holy name" (v. 22).

So from the priestly perspective, what will this gracious act of God look like? Certainly, the priests were concerned first with the uncleanness of idolatry and violence in the life of God's glory-bearing temple (i.e., the covenant community). For the priestly prophet Ezekiel, any resolution to this dilemma of life-taking uncleanness must involve some type of ritual of purification or cleansing of all that has become deathly or unclean. True to his priestly vision, Ezekiel understands that the temple, the land, and ultimately the people who occupy the temple and the land must be purged of the idols and the violence that have contaminated them. Temple, land, and people must be moved from unclean, life-taking, deathly agents to clean, life-giving, blessing agents. Through the priestly ritual of cleansing, they must be transformed *back into* what they were originally called to be—that is, not harbingers of death and destruction, but heralds of divine blessing to the world, bearers of the unique glory of their uniquely merciful, gracious, faithful, forgiving covenant God.

When we hear the priest's language of cleansing or purification in the mouth of Ezekiel, we really must be careful to remember what Ezekiel means. As we mentioned earlier, he does not have some kind of vague notion of a dirty, amorphous substance inside of a person or a community that must be cleaned out or cleaned off just as dirt is cleaned from a pair of pants. In fact, the priests, with Ezekiel being chief among them, are insistent that this uncleanness is directly attached to concrete actions such as idolatry and violence. The sacred cows, holy hills, and substitute kings have brought deathliness upon the people of God; the shed blood and social corruption have brought disease. Ezekiel adamantly insists, "You have become guilty by the blood that you have shed, and defiled by the idols that you have made" (22:4). He then expounds on what violent shed blood looks like:

Father and mother are treated with contempt in you; the alien residing within you suffers extortion; the or-

phan and the widow are wronged in you. You have de-
spised my holy things, and profaned my sabbaths. . . .
In you, they take bribes to shed blood; you take both
advance interest and accrued interest, and make gain of
your neighbors by extortion; and you have forgotten me,
says the Lord God. (Vv. 7-8, 12)

The glory-bearing covenant community has broken covenant with their covenant God through real-life, self-serving,
survival-oriented activities. And as a result, they have become death bearers, not life bearers; a curse, not a blessing.
That uncleanness must go; that impurity must be cleaned.

Reflecting the ritual of cleansing, Ezekiel poignantly
depicts how God himself as the high priest of this priestly people will carry out the familiar cleansing ritual as he
sprinkles clean water upon them (e.g., see Lev. 14:7). As a
result of this divinely initiated and divinely enacted ritual,
God announces to the people: "You shall be clean from all
your uncleannesses, and from all your idols I will cleanse
you" (Ezek. 36:25).

But a Resolution beyond Ritual

For Ezekiel, however, the people must undergo more
than a ritual of purification. Something has to occur alongside that ritual if the glory is ever to return, if the people
are ever going to be authentic glory bearers in the world.
It is here that Ezekiel begins to sound much like his contemporary who had remained back in the homeland during
the exile, Jeremiah. Perhaps it would be more appropriate
to say that both Ezekiel and Jeremiah echo the determination of God that something must be done beyond the reforms and commitments of the people (thus the traditional

prophetic voice) and beyond the rituals of purification and cleansing (thus the traditional priestly voice). Both prophetic and priestly visions of the God plot conceive a grand, transforming act of God. Something divinely initiated and divinely enacted must happen to the *leb*, the heart/mind.

Representing the pinnacle of the priestly voice, Ezekiel refuses to conclude with the ritual of purification. He recognizes that if the covenant people are to authentically be the glory-bearing means of divine blessing in the world, the way they think must change. Just as Jeremiah would speak of the *torah* or instruction of God being written upon the *leb* of the people, Ezekiel imagines a brand-new, transformed *leb*. It will no longer be the stubborn *leb* that refused to trust the Lord with undivided loyalty. It will no longer be the hardened *leb* that plays into the survival tactics of climbing holy hills, building sacred cows, and instituting substitute kings. It will no longer be the life-taking *leb* that overpowers one's neighbor to preserve his or her own life, possessions, and future. No, indeed, this *leb* will be flesh; it will be pliable, moldable, bending, trusting, and trustworthy. It will be life giving, not life taking.

Ezekiel goes even a step further. The Lord will not only transform the very *leb*, the thought processes and will, of the covenant people but also empower them to faithfully embody and flesh out their covenant identity. Just as Jeremiah speaks of the Lord's *torah*/instruction written on the minds of the people so that they think the Lord's way, Ezekiel anticipates that the very life-giving Spirit of God himself will move and motivate the people to live according to the ways of their covenant God. The same life-giving Spirit that hovered over the chaotic waters of creation and the flood, that empowered judges and prophets with divine strength and wisdom to carry out their tasks, that brought Ezekiel back to his feet after he fainted (Ezek. 1:28–2:2), and that ultimately will breathe upon the dead bones in the valley and resurrect them back into a mighty army (chap. 37)—that life-giving breath of God will cause the covenant people to follow and observe God's will. It is then—and only then—that the covenant people will truly and authentically be the covenant people: "Then . . . you shall be my people, and I will be your God" (36:28). As we have previously noted, in speaking of the same resolution, Jeremiah echoes Ezekiel: "I will put my law [*torah*] within them, and I will write it on their hearts [*leb*]; and I will be their God, and they shall be my people" (Jer. 31:33).

The God plot is about a people graciously called to covenant who tried again and again to be a people of undivided trust, undivided loyalty, to their God. But they were incapable! However, the God who called them is faithful and he himself will bring it about through a transformed heart/mind (*leb*). Indeed, the covenant God is determined: "I will be their God, and they shall be my people." There seems to be no more appropriate way to end this chapter than to once again repeat the blessing Paul gave to the church at Thessalonica: "May the God of peace [wholeness] himself sanctify you entirely [wholly]; and may your spirit and soul and body [the whole of who you are] be kept sound [complete] and blameless [whole] at the coming of our Lord Jesus Christ. *The one who calls you is faithful, and he will do this*" (1 Thess. 5:23-24, emphasis added).

PART III

The God Plot
A Transformed Mind

Within the setting of the gracious activities of the Lord's deliverance, provision, and covenant fidelity, the prophetic voice called the covenant people to undivided loyalty and untainted trust: "Love the LORD your God with *all* your heart, and with *all* your soul, and with *all* your [strength]" (Deut. 6:5, emphasis added). However, the covenant people faced a consistent struggle to trust the God who had graciously acted in their lives. That struggle was embodied in holy hills, sacred cows, and substitute kings. At first, the prophetic resolution to the human dilemma seemed to be in the people's commitment to reformation and renewal in their covenant with the Lord. However, one revival after another ended in a return to their same old ways. Clearly, something more than reform had to occur. As expressed in the prophet Jeremiah (see also Deut. 30), the only way the covenant people could ever authentically be devoted to and trust their covenant God undividedly was for something to happen to their way of thinking (heart/mind [*leb*]). Something had to be different about the way they imagined reality. If they were ever to live a life of complete trust in their covenant God, the *leb* itself must undergo transformation. In order to envision life differently, they must be captured by a *holy imagination*.

In a similar way, the priestly voice expressed the great dilemma in terms of sacred cows (idols), holy hills (other deities), and substitute kings (human powers), along with the tactics of survival against one's neighbor (violence). Because the priests were deeply committed to the agenda of life, all of these practices were viewed as contrary to God's unwavering commitment to life-giving blessing. Indeed, the priestly call had not been fulfilled by the covenant community: "Be holy, because I the LORD your God am holy" (see Lev. 11:44-45; 19:2; 20:7). The practices of idolatry and violence had made the people, the land, and the temple unclean (deathly rather than life giving). As a result, the covenant community was unable to carry out the task for which the covenant had been established from the start: blessed by God to be a blessing to the world, the community was to bear the tabernacling glory into the world.

From the priestly perspective, since the community had failed at its task, there was only one way for the God plot to reach its climax: the community, the land, and the temple had to again be made clean of idolatry and violence. However, as expressed through the prophet Ezekiel, the ultimate resolution went beyond the ritual of cleansing; the heart/mind (*leb*) must be transformed. If the covenant community was ever to bear the glory into the world so that the deadliest places on earth become filled with life, the stubborn, hard heart of survival must be transformed into a fleshy, trusting, faithful heart.

Both the prophetic and priestly voices meet in the climactic resolution to the human dilemma: a transformed mind. So what is this mind? Do we have any indications from the overarching plot of God what it might look like? We will explore the answers to these questions, along with other significant issues, in the following chapters.

nine

WITH EYES WIDE OPEN
THE VISION OF CHRIST,
THE MIND OF CHRIST

PERHAPS one of the most image-filled ways of describing the human mind is expressed in phrases such as, "Can't you see?" "Let me open your eyes for you." "I just need a new vision for this situation." Often the way we describe our minds or our way of thinking is through the language of seeing or envisioning.

This way of describing our understanding or mind-set is nothing new. To the prophet Isaiah, the Lord used the language of both seeing and hearing to describe the way the people of Israel just couldn't grasp or understand the prophetic message. In Isaiah's call, the Lord says to the prophet, "Go and say to this people, 'Keep listening, but do not comprehend; keep looking, but do not understand.' Make the mind of this people dull, and stop their ears, and shut their eyes" (Isa. 6:9-10). In the gospel of Mark, Jesus uses the same kind of language as Isaiah to describe the way the disciples just don't "get" Jesus at all. Jesus says to his disciples, "Do you still not perceive or understand? Are your hearts hardened? Do you have eyes, and fail to see? Do you have ears, and fail to hear? And do you not remember?" (8:17-18).

In Jesus' statement, we begin to realize that the disciples' dilemma of repeated fear as they follow Jesus will require so much more than changing their ways. If they are authentically to live as Jesus' disciples, their eyes have to be opened; their minds must be changed. Their whole way of thinking must be as radically altered as the eyes of a blind person who has regained his sight.

A Parable That Unlocks the Dilemma

The background of Jesus' statement concerning the blindness of his disciples in Mark 8 is fascinating. Soon after Jesus calls his disciples and appoints them to their mission (chaps. 1–3), he tells a parable that provides the key for understanding the entire gospel and ultimately for understanding the dilemma of the entire God plot: the parable of the farmer who sows seed (4:1-20). In the parable, we hear of seed that a farmer scatters along different types of soil. It apparently is all the same seed; likewise, the same farmer scatters the seed. However, the soil differs.

Some of the seed falls on the hard path. Before it even has a chance to get into the soil, the birds come and carry it away. In reading the gospel, the reader can't help but think of those hard-hearted (i.e., hard-minded) people embodied in the religious crowd of Pharisees and Sadducees. These people have the God they worship so figured out that when

Jesus speaks the good news, it has absolutely no chance of getting into their lives. Their minds are already made up.

Some of the seed falls into soil filled with thorns. Although the seed begins to sprout, the thorns around it smother it out. As Jesus interprets the thorns to be "the cares of the world, and the lure of wealth, and the desire for other things" (v. 19), one cannot help but think of characters like the rich young man who deeply desires the reign of God but who allows the accumulation of "possessions" to "choke out" the kingdom (v. 19; 10:17-31).

Still, some of the seed falls into what Jesus calls "good soil" (4:8). We really don't know just what composes good soil, but we do know that in this soil the seed sprouts, grows, and produces magnificently. Throughout the story of Jesus in the gospel of Mark, there are multiple examples of persons who hear the good news of the kingdom of God that Jesus announces. As they receive it into their lives through exorcisms, healings, and forgiveness, they just can't help but to spread the news of the kingdom. Even when Jesus has told them to keep quiet about what has happened, they run and tell everyone.

There is a fourth type of soil remaining in the parable. We have reserved our discussion of this soil till now because it is the focal point of the gospel of Mark. This soil depicts the followers of Jesus, the disciples. However, in this soil, we see not only the disciples during Jesus' ministry but also the great dilemma of the covenant community that we have been discussing throughout this book. Even more, in this soil we can look far into the future, far beyond Jesus' lifetime on earth, and see the perennial character of the church of Jesus Christ as it unfolds for the next twenty centuries. Jesus describes this soil—the soil of his disciples, the church, and the ancient covenant people called Israel—as rocky (Gk., *petros*) soil.

So what is this rocky soil like? It certainly is not a depiction of solid strength or steadfast fortitude. In fact, it is quite the opposite. Just as seed planted in rocky soil will often sprout very quickly, so does the seed of the gospel when it is planted in the followers of Jesus. They hear the declaration of Jesus and they "immediately" receive it with jubilation; the disciples "immediately" follow after Jesus (see 1:18-20). However, in rocky soil, plants cannot put down deep roots, and as a result they do not last long. Here is the grand dilemma of the covenant people within the God plot: the need to survive and the fear that emerges when survival is at risk! Whenever "trouble or persecution" comes, "*immediately* they fall away" (4:17, emphasis added). Although quick to follow, they are just as quick to disperse. One can only think of the person who often functioned as the pulse of Jesus' disciples—the true *petros*, Peter—and how quick he was to deny Jesus when threatened with persecution.

The Two-Sided Dilemma: Survival and Fear

It could be easy to conclude that this "quick to follow, quick to run" characteristic is simply a group mentality or personality trait of Jesus' disciples. However, the gospel of Mark is getting to something much deeper than groupthink or personality types. Soon after Jesus tells the parable of the different types of soil, a defining moment occurs in the life of his disciples. This incident provides an in-your-face hint that the disciples—or, even more, the people of God throughout the generations, both ancient Israel and the Christian church—are dealing with something much deeper than personality flaws or the herd mentality.

At the end of Mark 4, Jesus and his disciples cross to the other side of the sea in a boat. As they are crossing, a fierce storm breaks out. The mighty winds drive the waves up against the boat so that water begins to flow in. While Jesus continues to sleep through the storm, the disciples become overwhelmed with fear. Waking Jesus up from his sleep, they ask him, "Don't you even care that we are dying?" (see v. 38). After calming the chaotic waters, he asks his disciples the soul-searching question for all generations of the covenant community, both before and after the disciples: "Why are you afraid? Have you still no faith?" (v. 40).

This incident is only the beginning of what will become a characteristic problem: fear. To be precise, this is a fear that emerges out of a threat to one's survival. This paralyzing, debilitating fear is not a onetime event; it repeatedly appears in the life of Jesus' disciples (see 6:50; 9:32; 10:32); it becomes, or so it seems, their primary character trait. Even at the tomb, the good news of Jesus' resurrection is at first kept silent because of fear (16:8). The perennial dilemma for "rocky soil" is the fear that emerges from the deep-seated human compulsion to survive in the midst of trouble and persecution. When life is threatened, rocky soil—first-century disciples, pre-Christian Israel, the Christian church today—routinely becomes paralyzed by fear. This rocky soil then proceeds to scatter quickly away from God, taking the seed with it. As revealed throughout the God plot, the destination of this scattering is often the holy hills that promise growth, the sacred cows that promise answers, the substitute kings that promise victory, and the alternative alliances that promise protection.

No wonder one of the most repeated phrases in Scripture is this simple but complex declaration: "Do not be afraid"/"Fear not!" The phrase speaks into the life of the wandering, childless nomad Abram (Gen. 15:1) and to his son Isaac (26:24). It echoes on into a generation that finds itself wandering in the wilderness (Deut. 1:21) and paralyzed by its fear of giants (Num. 14:9). It challenges the next generation under a new leader, Joshua (Deut. 31:6, 8; Josh. 8:1; 10:8; 11:6). It echoes into the calls of Jeremiah (Jer. 1:8; 10:5) and Ezekiel (Ezek. 2:6) during the challenging days of destruction and defeat. It speaks to kings who fear invading armies (Isa. 7:4; 8:12). It echoes down into the tragic communal experience of exile (40:9; 41:10, 13, 14; 43:1, 5; 44:2, 8). It even speaks to the land and to the animals in times of massive devastation and overwhelming death (Joel 2:21-22). It comes from the mouths of heavenly messengers to the mother of Jesus (Luke 1:30), to Joseph (Matt. 1:20; Luke 1:13), and to shepherds (Luke 2:10). It comes from the mouth of the divine messenger to the apostle Paul, who is overwhelmed by the chaotic waters at sea (Acts 27:24).

The fear of the disciples in the midst of the storm at sea in Mark 4 only sets the stage for the reappearance of fear on the part of the disciples. Apparently it is going to take something much more than Jesus' declaration "Don't be afraid" to change their situation. The gospel of Mark has a fascinating way of demonstrating the way the disciples all too easily become frustrated and anxious. The same anxious fear reemerges in Mark 6:47-52 as an adverse wind arises on the sea. Once again, Jesus says to them, "Take heart, it is I; do not be afraid" (v. 50).

The disciples' fear arises again in a different setting. This time their experiences are remarkably similar to those in the life of ancient Israel. For both disciples and ancient Israel, the wilderness becomes the backdrop for fear and frustration over the same matter—no bread! It may be both coincidental and significant that the stories about the lack of bread in both cases occur in deserted, wilderness situations. Perhaps it is always in the desert, when we are most threatened, that we tend to see our deep-seated need to survive and become paralyzed by fear.

The bread stories of Jesus and his disciples begin one day when they are met by five thousand people in a desert area; there is no food to eat and no access to food. All the disciples have is five loaves of bread and two fish. Looking heavenward, Jesus "blessed and broke the loaves" (v. 41). Certainly the language sounds similar to the life-giving bread that he will break for his disciples in the upper room in Mark 14:22. With the blessed and broken bread, along with the fish, there is more than enough to go around. In fact, twelve baskets of leftovers remain. How fascinating that on the Jewish side of the Sea of Galilee, *twelve* baskets remain. More than enough is left to feed the Jewish population!

In spite of the incredible feeding of the five thousand, just a few days later the disciples seem to forget what Jesus had done. After Jesus and his disciples go over to the Gentile (non-Jewish) side of the Sea of Galilee, four thousand people show up. Once again, just like on the Jewish side of the sea, the crowd is hungry and has absolutely nothing to eat. Becoming characteristically anxious about the situation, the disciples ask Jesus, "How can one feed these people with bread here in the desert?" (8:4). Not only had they forgotten the defining story of their God who fed bread to their ancestors in the wilderness, but the disciples had also forgotten what happened just a couple days earlier. Once again, just as he had done on the Jewish side of the sea, Jesus takes the loaves, gives thanks, breaks them, and gives them. Once again, the pattern of language sounds amazingly similar to Mark 14:22 (see also 1 Cor. 11:23-24). Not only is everyone fed, but this time seven baskets remain. How fascinating—the Gentile number of perfection! Not only were enough baskets left over to feed the Jewish population (twelve), but enough baskets are also left over to feed the Gentile population (seven).

Now if the story ended here, it would be two great incidents of Jesus' provision *in the wilderness* for both Jews and Gentiles. But right after the second feeding, Jesus and his disciples are in a boat together. After the narrator tells us they had forgotten to bring any bread with them, the narrator makes a correction, saying, "They had only one loaf with them in the boat" (Mark 8:14). As Jesus warns his disciples to beware of the *yeast* of the Pharisees and of Herod, they once again live up to their fearful, survival-oriented way of thinking. They become anxious and frustrated. Having no idea what he means by "yeast," they conclude, "It is because we have no bread" (v. 16).

Finally, enough is enough for Jesus. He looks at his closed-minded, blind, deafened, fumbling, bumbling disciples and says, "Why are you talking about having no bread? Do you still not perceive or understand? Are your hearts hardened? Do you have eyes, and fail to see? Do you have ears, and fail to hear?" (vv. 17-18). After reminding them of the leftover bread for both the five thousand and the four thousand, he once again says in what appears to be amazement and bewilderment on the part of Jesus, "Do you not yet understand?" (v. 21).

After all that his disciples had witnessed, one might think that Jesus would simply tell his disciples, "Just go back home! I'll go select twelve more people to follow me." However, Jesus understands what a disciple truly is—a learner, a follower, one who is tutored by a mentor. So rather than giving up on his disciples who "just don't get it," he takes them on a journey—a journey all the way to Jerusalem. In the process, he hopes to open their eyes, to transform their vision, to change their minds. In this mind-transforming, eye-opening journey, it is possible to hear echoes of the prophetic and priestly voices of the God plot—the voices that dared to imagine a new *leb*, a transformed way of thinking.

The Discipleship Journey to Jerusalem: Eye Opening, Mind Transforming

The journey on which Jesus takes his disciples begins and ends with an eye-opening experience—literally. Two stories of Jesus' healing blind men provide the prelude and the postlude to his attempts to open the eyes (or minds) of his disciples. In Mark 8:22-26, Jesus opens a blind man's eyes in a way that, although being odd, leaves the impression he wants on the vision (or minds) of his disciples. The journey ends in Mark 10 with Jesus' opening blind Bartimaeus's eyes. Tucked between the bookends of these eye-opening experiences is the ultimate eye-opening, mind-transforming experience that Jesus wants for the life of his disciples.

He is deeply committed not only to his disciples having eyes and ears but also to their being able to see and understand.

The opening story of a blind man in Mark 8:22-26 has to be one of the oddest of all the miracle stories of Jesus. It brings to mind an eye doctor adjusting the lenses on a Phoroptor (the multilensed, lung-shaped device that patients look through) to determine a person's eyeglass prescription. As he or she clicks through different lenses, an eye doctor can seem like a miracle worker, taking a person's eyesight from blurry vision to vision that is completely clear. In this story, Jesus—the divine Optometrist—is doing something very similar with the blind man and then with his disciples in the journey that follows.

At first, Jesus spits on the man's eyes and asks him if he sees anything. The man answers that he sees people, but the people look like trees walking around. The "walking trees" probably aren't referring to people with exotically colored hairstyles! The man who was once completely blind is now able to see people; however, he cannot see people clearly. Then Jesus proceeds to touch the man's eyes a second time. At this point, one can almost hear the *click, click, click* of the Phoroptor. After the divine Optometrist does his work, everything becomes clear, crisp, precise! The man who was once blind and then who regained partial vision finally exclaims, "I see everything clearly!" (see v. 25). In this strange event, we can't help but hear the words that Jesus has just spoken to his disciples, "Do you have eyes, and fail to see?" (v. 18). This odd healing of the blind man sets the stage for Jesus' attempt to move his disciples from a vision of him and his kingdom that is fuzzy to a vision that is clear.

In Mark 8:27, the followers of Jesus, both then and now, step into the office of the divine Optometrist. Jesus first tests for complete "blindness" by asking his disciples the question, "Who do people say that I am?" In other words, "How do people see me?" The response he gets demonstrates a complete blindness on the part of the masses. The crowds seem to be oblivious, blind, to anything about the true identity of Jesus. Some would say he is John the Baptist, while others say he is Elijah, yet others describe him as one of the other prophets. To many, he is, indeed, another prophet, a preacher, a reformer, an outspoken enemy of the political and economic system.

The divine Optometrist then proceeds to test the vision of his disciples. Surely they have been with him long enough to see him for who he really is. With the backdrop of a *click, click, click,* Jesus asks them, "What about you? How do you see me? Who do you say that I am?" (see v. 29). On behalf of the other disciples, and for that matter on behalf of the Christian church, Peter gives his vision of Jesus as he exclaims, "You are the Messiah" (v. 29). The disciples—and Peter in particular—have been with Jesus long enough to recognize that he is somehow the One who will establish the kingdom of God. He is the long-anticipated Messiah.

As Jesus and his disciples are on the road to Jerusalem, the confession of Peter (and the church) begins to make sense. In Peter's mind, Jesus and his disciples are on their way to the religious and political capital to overthrow the present political and religious system and to establish the reign of God by crowning Jesus as king—as Messiah.

In the light of Peter and the disciple's vision of Jesus up to this point, Peter's confession just seems right. But based on the remainder of the journey, Peter's confession is eerily similar to the blind man who saw people, but they looked like walking trees. The disciples, particularly Peter, have been with Jesus long enough to be able to say that Jesus is all about establishing the reign of God. While at least having some type of vision, the disciples' vision remains amazingly blurry. In fact, Peter's vision is so blurry that he will still become terrified when storms spring up on the lake, when Jesus comes walking on the water, and eventually when strangers identify him as a follower of Jesus so that out of fear and intimidation he will deny even knowing Jesus. Indeed, he lives up to his name—*Petros*, "Rocky." He is quick to follow and quick to confess, but when troubles come, he is quick to wither away in fear.

Jesus, the divine Optometrist, proceeds immediately to bring some clarity to Peter's confession. Jesus will do this "clearing of vision" three times during the journey to Jerusalem (8:31-38; 9:30-37; 10:32-45). In each incident, Jesus talks to his disciples about going to Jerusalem, suffering, dying, and rising again. In response to Jesus' words about suffering and dying, the disciples will demonstrate their "blurry vision" of Jesus as they say things and do things that demonstrate that they just don't really see things clearly. However, each of the three times that the disciples show "blurred vision," Jesus does not give up on his fear-filled, half-blind disciples. Instead, he does exactly what master teachers will most often do with their students. He teaches and transforms; he clears their eyes; he opens their minds to a crisp, precise vision. This is discipleship at its best as it is led by the Master Teacher in the hope that his disciples will ultimately see "everything clearly" (see 8:25).

discipleship

As soon as Jesus finishes his words on suffering and dying in Jerusalem in chapter 8, Peter, the very one who has just declared Jesus to be the Messiah, rushes to try to correct Jesus. Better yet, he *rebukes* Jesus—exactly what Jesus has been doing with demons up to now (see 9:25). Apparently Peter seems to think that something has gone awry in Jesus' vision, and he must set out to clarify Jesus' understanding. Surely Jesus' mind has become muddled, so Peter must clear up Jesus' thinking on the matter.

However, it is now Jesus who will clear up Peter's thinking and clarify his vision. With an optometrist's *click, click, click* in the background, the divine Optometrist, Jesus, begins to clear the vision of Peter and the other disciples. Jesus says, "If any want to become my followers, let them deny themselves and take up their cross and follow me" (8:34). With an added *click, click, click,* the divine Optometrist proceeds by saying, "Those who want to save their life will lose it, and those who lose their life for my sake, and for the sake of the gospel, will save it" (v. 35).

Wow! There is the perennial struggle we have had all along as the covenant people—survival, that is, seeking to preserve our own lives, ministries, families, and institutions. Over and over again, the dilemma of survival leads us to climb the holy hills, to build the sacred cows, to seek alternative kings to fight our battles, and to ally ourselves with powers and principalities to protect us. But once we have climbed the highest hill and performed so well for a good tip; once we have constructed the sturdiest idol that can contain God or any other provider; once we have instituted the "sure king" who can overcome our fiercest, most threatening enemy; and once we have allied with the most reliable political and economic partners, the hills crumble, the idols fall, the kings die, the alliances disintegrate—and so do we!

Now the divine Optometrist is giving one more click in the eye-opening journey of discipleship. Life is more than survival. To live in order to save our lives, ministries, reputations, and institutions we hold so dear is the beginning of our end. To seek to survive is to die, but to die for the sake of the good news of the undivided reign of God is to discover life. But this is a whole new way of understanding. It is a whole new way of seeing things. It is a whole new way of thinking and living. It is cleared eyes; it is transformed vision; it is a new mind. I guess we could actually call it *the mind of Christ*.

But the discipleship journey does not end with a few clicks. It continues. The discipleship journey never receives a diploma. It is committed to staying with Jesus all the way to Jerusalem—and beyond. Once again, in Mark 9:30-37, Jesus starts talking about the suffering, death, and resurrection that is about to take place in Jerusalem. This time the disciples show just how blurry their vision is. At least, in the earlier events of chapter 8, Peter seemed to hear Jesus. This time, the disciples seem so engaged in thinking other thoughts that they do not even hear the words of Jesus as he talks about death and suffering. This time, they argue among themselves: "Which of us is the greatest?" (see 9:34). It seems that across the centuries, the argument has not changed much. Who is the greatest in the workplace? In the church? In the home? What's the greatest church in the community? Is it the one with the biggest building, the most people, or the most vibrant worship music?

Honestly, the argument on the way to Jerusalem is probably not an argument about who is number one. For the disciples, they really did perceive their teacher, Jesus, as Number One, or at least they would have said so. They attempted to confess that he was the King, the Christ. Their struggle, as well as the struggle of Jesus' followers throughout time, has more precisely been over who is number two and number three. Who is the greatest?

Some teachers may finally tell a student who just can't "get it" to "get out," but not Jesus. Once again, he really is the Master Teacher. He really is the tenacious Optometrist no matter how blurry the vision of his disciples might become. With another *click, click, click,* the eye-opening, transforming Healer begins to clarify their vision as he says, "Whoever wants to be first must be last of all and servant of all" (v. 35). Now some of us may understand this idea of the first being last and the last first differently from the way Jesus intended. We may think that in this lifetime, we must seek to be last and least of all. We must let others get ahead of us, and we must take the back of the line. Yet, all the while, we believe deeply that a future afterlife awaits us when we will be moved in the blink of an eye from the back to the front of the line, from the low end to the high end of the heavenly banquet table. Suddenly, we will be first! Then we can look at all of those behind us in eternity and say, "Gotcha! The first will be last and the last will be first."

But if we consider carefully what Jesus is saying, we will find that for him the idea of some sort of heavenly promotion following a life of earthly demotion is a completely alien way of thinking. From Jesus' perspective, there is no delayed response in putting the least at the high end of a heavenly banquet table or moving the last to the front of the line. For Jesus, there is a whole other way of seeing things. For him, to be least, last, or a servant is actually in and of itself to be great or first, not some day in the future, but right now, in the here and now. What a remarkably alternative way of seeing reality! The only way we could ever get into something like this, the only way we could ever even begin to believe something so alternative, is for our eyes to be opened. The only way is through a transformed way of thinking, a new mind—the mind of Jesus.

The journey of Jesus and his disciples continues toward Jerusalem. To be on the road with Jesus does not lead to graduation; it leads to transformation. Just as we saw in Mark 8:31 and again in 9:31, Jesus continues talking about his imminent suffering, death, and resurrection in 10:33-34. This time, he goes into even greater detail than previously. However, just as the other two times, the disciples who have been following Jesus just long enough to confess that he is the Messiah reveal their blurry vision about him. This time, James and John specifically reveal their misunderstanding of Jesus by the special request they make of him. After they ask Jesus to do for them whatever they request, Jesus replies with an answer any of us would love to hear from him: "What is it you want me to do for you?" (v. 36). Their response shows just how unclear their vision of Jesus is: "Grant us to sit, one at your right hand and one at your left, in your glory" (v. 37). In other words, "When you are crowned King—when you are anointed as the Messiah— please let us be the 'vice-kings,' the second in command." Again, we see clearly that the challenge followers of Jesus have often faced is not in their attempts at being number one (the indisputable status of Jesus); it is in their attempts to be number two and number three.

The problem with the request of James and John (and us as well) is that they (we) "just don't get it." We just don't see and think the way Jesus sees and thinks. Jesus' response makes clear just how unclear James and John's request is: "You do not know what you are asking. Are you able to drink the cup that I drink, or be baptized with the baptism that I am baptized with?" (v. 38).

The two disciples' blurry vision becomes all the more evident in their response: "We are able" (v. 39). As the other ten disciples of Jesus become outraged over the self-serving request of James and John, Jesus, the divine Optometrist, once again attempts to bring sharpness to their vision. Once again, the patient Instructor and persistent Eye Doctor refuses to give up on his blurry-eyed, narrow-minded, "rocky" disciples. Rather than abandoning them or telling them to give up on the journey, this determined divine Optometrist provides yet again a *click, click, click*. Indeed, this road with Jesus is the journey of discipleship. The eye-opening, mind-transforming Healer sharpens their vision as he says, "You know that among the Gentiles those whom they recognize as their rulers lord it over them, and their great ones are tyrants over them. But it is not so among you; but whoever wishes to become great among you must be your servant, and whoever wishes to be first among you must be slave of all. For the Son of Man came not to be served but to serve, and to give his life a ransom for many" (vv. 42-45).

What an ironic request! "Grant us to sit, one at your right hand and one at your left, in your glory" (v. 37). There is only one place in the gospel where there is one person on

Jesus' right and another person on Jesus' left. Indeed, it is the only time that Jesus will be acclaimed, albeit in mockery, "King of the Jews!" We find this account in Mark 15, which says, "And with him they crucified two bandits, one on his right and one on his left" (v. 27). No wonder he would say to James and John, "You do not know what you are asking" (10:38). They just couldn't *see* it. Their minds could not comprehend it. They knew he was the Messiah, but they had no idea what this Messiah was thinking. If they ever were to think this way, they indeed must have the very mind of Christ. The words of Jesus to his disciples at the very beginning of the journey to Jerusalem echo forward, "Do you still not perceive or understand? . . . Do you have eyes, and fail to see? Do you have ears, and fail to hear? . . . Do you not yet understand?" (8:17-18, 21).

What Kind of Mind Is This? More than Survival

Certainly the disciples' fear on the stormy sea was not unique to them. The anxiety that would cause them to deny a suffering Messiah, to argue over their own greatness, and to seek positions of prestige and authority is not unusual in the life of the people of God. The same fear and anxiety that gripped the disciples underlay the Israelites' construction of sacred cows, their habitual journeys up holy hills, and their resolute demand for substitute kings. They—no we— are scared to death of not surviving. The sea will drown us. The darkness will overwhelm us. The enemies will crush us. The famine will starve us. Fear and anxiety that arise from our desire to survive motivate us, just as they motivated our ancestors, to climb holy hills, build sacred cows, and call for substitute kings.

Now we finally are getting to the dilemma behind the dilemma. Only on the surface is the dilemma our creation of idols, our loyalty to the gods/powers of our culture, and our creation of political, economic, and religious systems to fight our battles and save our lives. Just as our Israelite ancestors, we can resolve to change; we can offer more sacrifices, burn our idols, throw away our false gods, overthrow our kings, and dissolve our alliances. But in our drive to survive, we become terrified when our lives and self-made worlds are threatened. So once again, we build new idols or resurrect old ones, climb the holy hills, and seek one more king or alliance to save us. Like the Israelites, we are caught up in the continuous cycle of reform and relapse for the sake of survival.

So what is the alternative way of "seeing"? What does Jesus' *vision* or *mind* look like? It is a vision that does not exist to survive but to give. It is a mind that does "nothing from selfish ambition or conceit" (Phil. 2:3). It is a mind that does not look to our "own interests, but to the interests of others" (v. 4). It is a mind that empties itself, takes "the form of a slave," humbles itself, and becomes "obedient to the point of death—even death on a cross" (vv. 7-8). It is a mind that does not hold on to life in order to survive but relinquishes it in order that others might live.

So, What Do You Want Me to Do for You?

What a haunting question from Jesus is his response to the two brothers asking him to do whatever they request: "What is it you want me to do for you?" (Mark 10:36). "Grant us to sit, one at your right hand and one at your left, in your glory" (v. 37). If survival is in the mind of Jesus, their request makes complete sense. If Jesus understood the use of power to be for the sake of self-preservation, then the disciples' request is perfect. If the fear of the loss of our own life, power, or prestige is the motivating force behind our lives, then their request is right on target. But weren't survival, self-preservation, and the fear of the loss of life, power, and prestige also the driving forces behind holy hills, sacred cows, and substitute kings?

On the other hand, if the mind of Jesus understands that life is lived not for the sake of oneself but for the sake of the other, then the request makes no sense. If the use of power is not for the sake of self-preservation but for the sake of extending life to the other person, then the request is utterly flawed. If fear of loss is not the motivating force behind our lives but rather trust in the God who graciously delivers, provides, and makes covenant, then their request has missed the target completely.

So maybe the heart of the disciples' dilemma really is a misunderstanding—a dim vision—of what it means for Jesus to come into his glory. Maybe from the start, not only the disciples but also the people of God throughout history have been blind to what the glory of God really is. Perhaps the glory bearers were bearing a misunderstood glory all along. What if that brilliant, blinding light of God's otherness is not raw power that seeks to save itself? What if it does not desire to use its power for self-exaltation and self-preservation? What if Jesus' coming into his glory is indeed the very glory of God? What if that glory really is mercy, grace, slowness to anger, abounding steadfast love, faithfulness, and forgiveness (see Exod. 34:6-7 and our discussion in chapter 5)? What if the disciples have such a partial vision of the glory of God that they could never begin to imagine what it would look like for Jesus to come into his glory?

"What is it you want me to do for you?" (Mark 10:36). What a question to disciples whose eyes are opened just enough to confess that Jesus is Messiah but whose vision is so foggy that they can't see him clearly. Having blind eyes is equivalent to having blind minds. Likewise, having blurry eyes is the same as having blurry minds. Then blind Bartimaeus steps in (vv. 46-52). What a way for this journey of the disciples to end. Bartimaeus, the blind beggar, begins to shout out, "Jesus, Son of David, have mercy on me!" (v. 47). In spite of the hurdles thrown in his way, he remains persistent as he cries out all the more loudly, "Son of David, have mercy on me!" (v. 48). As Jesus calls Bartimaeus to him, he asks the blind beggar, "What do you want me to do for you?" (v. 51). Does this question sound familiar? As the same question Jesus asked James and John resounds now into the blind beggar's life, the beggar responds, "My teacher, let me see again" (v. 51). And "immediately he regained his sight and followed [Jesus] on the way" (v. 52).

As we reflect on this journey of discipleship that began in Bethsaida in Mark 8:22, we cannot help but recall the eye-opening/mind-changing incident that set the context. "Then Jesus laid his hands on his eyes again; and he looked intently and his sight was restored, *and he saw everything clearly*" (v. 25, emphasis added).

"What do you want me to do for you?" The same question with two remarkably contrasting answers: "Put us on your right and left" or "Let me see." The request to sit on

Jesus' *right and left* is not granted; however, the request to *see* is! "Let me see!"—what a remarkable prayer to be prayed by disciples who have heard their Master Teacher ask, "Do you have eyes but fail to see? Do you still not understand?" (see vv. 17-18).

How Can Vision Be Cleared? How Can the Mind Be Transformed?

In our journey through the God plot, we have come to see that the great dilemma of the people of God is ultimately not the idols they construct, the hills they climb, the kings they establish, or the alliances they build. At the core of the dilemma is the human dilemma: survival through self-preservation. This self-preservation can be individual, but it is often systemic in communities, societies, and institutions, just as it was in the communal life of our biblical ancestors. All the reform in the world cannot change this mind-set. Even when we change our ways, our vision remains blurry and our minds remain stubbornly convinced that in order to survive our giants, the battle is ours to fight; in order to survive our hunger and thirst, the meal is ours to prepare; and in order to save our lives, the alliance is ours to make.

Can we ever begin to imagine our lives beyond survival and self-preservation? Can we ever begin to imagine our lives as self-giving love for the sake of the other, as life-giving blessing from the life-giving God? Can we ever trust this delivering, providing, covenanting God in such a way that we do not revert back to our survival-oriented sacred cows, holy hills, substitute kings, and life-preserving alliances? Can our partial vision ever be restored so that we can see things clearly? Can our divided minds/hearts ever be transformed so that we can indeed remain loyal to (love) the Lord with *all* of our heart, *all* of our soul, and *all* of our strength? Or are we doomed to dim vision and divided minds?

It is all too easy to remain paralyzed by the evidences of the human dilemma that we have observed throughout history. It really does seem that from generation to generation, we are stuck in the survival, self-preservation mode. We make our home in the real world of the human dilemma in which even religious individuals and institutions seek more to preserve their lives from others than to lose their lives for others. Perhaps we have become so accustomed to the human dilemma of survival through trusting only ourselves that we have lost any sense of holy imagination.

What might this holy imagination look like? Perhaps it looks like Moses' daring repeated calls to the people of God to love the Lord with *all* their heart/mind (*leb*). Perhaps this holy imagination looks like Moses' anticipation that the Lord himself would circumcise the *leb* of the people so that they then would be enabled to love the Lord with all their heart and soul. Perhaps it looks like Jeremiah's courage in the face of repeated failures on the part of the people to imagine that God's instruction (*torah*) would eventually be written upon the very *leb* of God's people. Perhaps that holy imagination looks like the boldness of Ezekiel to imagine that God could take a stubborn, stony *leb* that repeatedly climbs hills, builds idols, and establishes kings and transform it to a faithful, fleshy *leb* that is moved by the very Spirit of God so that the people would faithfully and wholeheartedly trust in the Lord. Perhaps that holy imagination looks like the audacity of Jesus to imagine that the repeated call to love the Lord with *all* the heart, *all* the soul, *all* the mind, and *all* the strength and to love one's neighbor as oneself had not ended because of the people's failure but rather was the greatest commandment. Perhaps that holy imagination looks like Paul's audacious declaration "We have the mind of Christ" (1 Cor. 2:16) and bold invitation "Let the same mind be in you that was in Christ Jesus" (Phil. 2:5).

But how? How does this vision of Jesus, this mind of Christ, ever begin to take shape in our lives? The eye-opening, mind-changing journey we have just explored helps us to imagine the way this transformation begins to occur. The very nature of the eye opening of both blind men was entirely an act of God; it was complete miracle. The blind men could not restore their own sight. No matter how hard the blind men might try, their eyes would remain shut. Eye-opening, mind-transforming activity is 100 percent God; it is 100 percent divine grace.

Tucked between the two eye-opening accounts is the journey Jesus makes with his disciples. As Jesus instructs, explains, and answers their questions *on the way* to Jerusalem, they begin to see things more clearly. Light not only breaks into their vision. The light of understanding begins to burst forth upon the disciples' minds. No wonder one of the earliest names for the Jesus movement was "the Way" (Acts 24:14). To be a follower of Jesus is to be on the road (the way) with Jesus and with fellow disciples; it is a journey for our vision and minds to be transformed to the vision and mind of Jesus. Perhaps the apostle Paul most beautifully articulated this journey as he wrote to the church at Corinth: "All of us, with unveiled faces, seeing the glory of the Lord as though reflected in a mirror, are being transformed into the same image from one degree of glory to another; for this comes from the Lord, the Spirit" (2 Cor. 3:18).

Paul is firmly convinced that this activity is from the very Spirit of God himself. No matter how hard we try, we cannot open our own blind eyes or clear our own dim vision. The eye-opening, mind-changing activity is the activity of God. But the God who calls us to this transformed mind—to love and to trust him undividedly, to be his glory bearers—that God "is faithful, and he will do this" (1 Thess. 5:24).

As we discovered earlier, as far back as Moses' message in Deuteronomy, the Source of this transformed way of thinking is clear. Recognizing that the people would be absolutely unable through their own reforms and "self-helps" to change their ways, Moses anticipated that the Lord would "circumcise" the "heart" (*leb*) of the people and the "heart" (*leb*) of their descendants (30:6). As we also observed, Jeremiah likewise imagined the Source of transformation, declaring that God would put his instruction or "law" (*torah*) within his people and would "write it on their hearts [*leb*]" (Jer. 31:33). Thus the God plot read in its entirety—beginning with the hope and anticipation of people such as Moses and Jeremiah—imagines more! It dreams more! It hopes more! Moreover, the God who calls his people to a clear vision, a transformed mind, will faithfully and surely bring it about.

Sounds great, right? So does all of this emphasis on God as the Source of mind transformation and on divine grace as the stimulus of the Christ vision mean that we, the people of God, the disciples of Jesus, should sit passively, waiting for God to transform our minds? The answer is tentatively yes—provided we sit as passively as the disciples did when they traveled with Christ *on the way* to Jerusalem. How passive is that? When he graciously invites us to join him *on the way*, we are to do just that—we are to join him *on the way*. And while we are on the way, an authentic cooperation with the eye-opening, mind-changing Christ will begin to take place as he himself graciously acts. Through the opportunities he graciously provides, we will experience a genuine, real interaction between his life, death, and resurrection and our own lives. We participate in these opportunities or *disciplines* of the Christian life *by faith*, daring to believe that they provide a means by which God's grace continues to open our eyes to the Christ vision and to transform our minds to the mind of Christ. And indeed, on the way, he does graciously and miraculously open our eyes; he transforms our *leb*.

Richard Foster has rightly observed that these opportunities or disciplines of the Christian life "can do nothing" by themselves; however, as instruments of God's transforming grace they become "the means by which we place ourselves where [God] can bless us."[1] What do these opportunities look like? Though they can take on different appearances from generation to generation, these opportunities include our wholehearted engagement in the following:

- Participating in authentic dialogue/prayer with God— speaking to him and hearing him speak back to us
- Participating in a life of confession—seeing Jesus and seeing ourselves and naming the difference
- Participating in actively listening to the voice of God through hearing and reading Scripture—engaging in the God plot as it unfolds in the Scripture that has been handed to us by the people of God

- Participating in seeing him and responding to him through corporate worship
- Participating in the broken body and shed blood of Jesus Christ through Holy Communion and in his death and resurrection through Christian baptism
- Participating in the authentic life of the body of Christ—the people of God—through genuine fellowship and honest accountability
- Participating in the acts of mercy in which Christ would engage—showing up where he already is at work and joining him there

ten

TO TOUCH A LEPER
MORE THAN SURVIVAL!

SO WHAT does an undivided mind, an unadulterated heart (*leb*), look like when it puts on flesh and blood? What would a mind look like that exists not to save its own life but to give of itself for the lives of others? What would a community of people look like who see themselves as a kingdom of priests and a holy nation, glory bearers to the world, and life givers rather than life takers?

Although both the prophetic and the priestly voices celebrated God's gracious deliverance from oppression and provision in the barren wilderness, the priestly voice particularly emphasized the *why* behind this gracious activity of God. The priests were concerned with how divine deliverance, provision, and covenant translated into the role or purpose of the people of God in the world. They were convinced that God was on a mission in the world. His attention was centered on creation, going to the lifeless places and bringing blessing, to the darkest places and bringing light, and to the most hopeless places and bringing a tomorrow.

For the priests, the creative, life-giving work of God was set into motion in the opening chapters of the Bible, but that work continued from generation to generation. Thus they were absolutely convinced that the covenant community was now to participate cooperatively with their covenant God in his divine mission of creative, life-giving deliverance and provision. They understood the role of God's covenant community to be a synergistic partnership with the creative, life-giving God. Only God himself was the gracious Life Giver, but the priestly covenant community was his partnering instrument or means through which he would breathe life into his world. For the priests, deliverance, provision, and covenant were now to be translated from the community's confession of what God had done for them into a lifestyle of life-giving deliverance, provision, and covenantal relationships in their world.

The priests were guided by a conviction that their covenant God was in no way a micromanager who would do this life-giving mission alone. They understood their own role as priests in the community as a partnership with God in his life-giving, creative role. Just as God had empowered life with blessing at the end of the creation story and after the disastrous, life-taking flood (Gen. 1:22, 28; 9:1) and just as God empowered Abram and Sarai with life, fertility, and hope by speaking blessing upon their lives and the life of their family (12:2), the priests took seriously their role of speaking God's life-giving blessing upon the people of God: "The LORD bless you and keep you; the LORD make his face to shine upon you, and be gracious to you; the LORD lift up his countenance upon you, and give you peace" (Num. 6:24-26).

The priests understood their role of blessing as a paradigm for the priestly role of the covenant community in relationship to the world and to all creation. Just as the priests were the instruments of God's blessing to the covenant community, so the covenant community was the instrument of God's blessing to the world. No wonder in the opening verses of God's promise to Israel's ancestors, God would say to Abram, "You will be a blessing. . . . and in you all the families of the earth shall be blessed" (Gen. 12:2-3).

As we have seen, not only did the priests understand themselves as instruments of God's life-giving blessing in their community, but they also were concerned with various behaviors, even various foods, that were especially life giving or life taking. Whatever promoted life, from certain actions to certain foods, they labeled as clean. Whatever took life, from various activities to specific foods and animals, they labeled as unclean.

They were especially concerned about preventing the transfer of disease and deathliness from one member of the community to another. It shouldn't really seem all that strange to us, even several millennia later, that they were so concerned about the spread of disease and death through bodily fluids. Just as a parent might instruct a child to cover his or her mouth when the child coughs in order to avoid contaminating others in the family, so the priests instructed the community on how to avoid contamination of healthy persons (clean) by unhealthy persons (unclean).

In this cooperative mission of life, there is a very fine line that can begin to emerge. The "pro-life" stance can easily move from an offensive position, the bestowal of blessing or the giving of life, to a defensive position, the retention of blessing or life by avoiding the diseased or deathly. It is such a fine line, and it is so easy to slip from life givers to "life preservers." In fact, it is easy even for the people of God unwittingly, even unknowingly, to shift the mission of God from life giving (blessing) to life preserving (curse). In this subtle shift, speaking curses against threats to life becomes the mission instead of speaking blessings into deathly places and situations.

This subtle shift or slow drift away from pro-life to anti-death often occurs when the people of God feel most threatened. It becomes all too easy to take up rocks and sticks to defeat deathliness rather than to continue speaking blessing and life into disease, deathliness, and disaster. When we are threatened, curse seems to get an upper hand over blessing.

Indeed, in time, the priestly voice began to understand its role as saving life or preserving life over that of giving life. Before we go pointing fingers, this drift is easy to understand. If one's focus is life, then protecting the living from the dead can easily become the emphasis. In the name of life, guarding the living from deathliness can even become one's reason for existence. With their cooperation in the divine agenda of life, the priests often concluded that healthy people should avoid sick people, living bodies should avoid dead bodies, and, by all means, healthy people should avoid any bodily fluids that could contaminate or even kill. This approach just makes sense: when unclean things or people touch clean things or people, they make the clean things or people unclean. But the opposite effect is next to impossible: when a clean thing or person touches an unclean thing or person, the clean does not make the unclean clean. The priestly prophet Haggai said almost the same thing when he was conversing with fellow priests: clean things do not make dirty things clean, but dirty things definitely make clean things dirty (see Hag. 2:11-13). Why then would a healthy person want any physical contact with an unhealthy person if life were the goal? A person would risk his or her health, even his or her life.

Into the middle of this growing priestly conviction enters a prophet-priest whose teaching had a completely different vision of life and death, clean and unclean, holy and unholy. He would make statements that made complete sense on the surface, yet underneath, those statements sharply contrasted with the priestly understanding of life and death. He taught, for example, "Those who are well have no need of a physician, but those who are sick" (Mark 2:17). It really does make sense that a physician's primary responsibility is not to protect those who are healthy but to bring healing to those who are sick. Yet this commonsense statement rearranged the primary role of priests and priestly communities from being about preserving the healthy and celebrating the living to being about healing the sick and speaking resurrection to the dead. Through stories he told about lost sheep being found, lost coins being discovered, and runaway sons coming home, he made it clear that his focus was more on the diseased, the lost, the dead, and the runaway rebel than on the healthy, the secure, the living, and the stay-at-home child (Luke 15).

His teachings and stories made his vision of clean and unclean, life and death, readily apparent. However, it was his lifestyle and actions that put flesh and blood to those teachings. He didn't just talk about an alternative understanding of clean and unclean, of life and death. He fleshed it out. He embodied it in whom or what he touched and where he went.

How much more obvious can this radically alternative vision, this unique (holy) mind, be than when the leper, oozing with bodily fluids, came to Jesus begging him to make him *clean* (Mark 1:40-42)? Moved with compassion, Jesus said to the leper, "I do choose [to do this]. Be made clean!" (v. 41). Really now, the words should have and could have been enough, but they were not for Jesus. For the unclean man to be clean, an action accompanied Jesus' words: he "stretched out his hand *and touched him*" (v. 41, emphasis added). What a risk! What danger! Jesus surely didn't put a glove on before reaching out to the man. And it's certainly unlikely that he went and poured half a bottle of hand sanitizer on himself afterward. He risked disease—uncleanness—in order to make this man whole and clean.

Survival was not Jesus' focus; life and healing were. His mind was different. He imagined an alternative to protective security, to hoarding, to carpe diem, and ultimately to self-survival. He imagined that clean can touch unclean and the unclean will become clean. He imagined that as life touches deathliness, deathliness is brought to life and wholeness. His vision was a different vision; his mind, an alternative mind; and his imagination, a holy imagination! By taking on death, this afflicted man might live! Cleanness, life, wholeness, is infectious. Holiness is contagious. How different, how alternative—how holy!

The thread of this alternative vision, this holy imagination, continues with the synagogue leader, Jairus, falling at Jesus' feet and begging Jesus to come to his house and heal his dying little girl (5:21-43). On the journey to Jairus's house, in the crowd pressing in on Jesus, there was a woman who had been hemorrhaging for twelve years. Blood, bodily fluid outside of the body, unclean, deathly—surely this was someone to avoid at all costs! Or maybe not? The woman dared to imagine—to hope—that if only she could touch or *be touched* by Jesus' garment, she would be made clean. She would be given healing, hope, and life. Realizing that life itself had gone out from him, Jesus exclaimed, "Who touched my clothes?" (v. 30). As she fell in fear before him and explained her reasoning, he responded, "Go in peace, and be healed of your disease" (v. 34). When the unclean touches the clean, the unclean becomes clean.

Finally arriving at Jairus's home, Jesus made his way into the room of the now deceased little girl. In the midst of the stench of death and the deathly commotion of wails and grief, Jesus "took her by the hand and said to her, . . . 'Little girl, get up!'" (v. 41). Did you catch it? "He took her by the hand." He had the audacity to enact *contagious cleanness*. He imagined differently—a holy imagination—as "he took her by the hand." He contaminated death with life by putting his own life on the line. He infected disease with healing by risking his own health.

A leper, a hemorrhaging woman, and a dead girl—in it all, Jesus had such a different *priestly* understanding of life and death, clean and unclean. Like the priests before him, he knew that the God plot was about life. But the distinction of his priestly perspective came down to this question: was the divine agenda of life carried out by avoiding death or by risking, even taking on, death so that life might be given? Perhaps unwittingly, even unknowingly at first, the priests had developed a myopic vision of life and death. The sick were to be shunned so that they would not affect the healthy, and the dead were to be avoided so that they would not contaminate the living. Life was to be preserved at all costs to prevent death.

However, the imagination of Jesus Christ was so other. It was so different (holy) from the widely held priestly view and practice. What if risking life by taking on death, by touching the most diseased and deadly corpses around us, by being touched by the flow of contaminated blood, by embracing the oozing sores and peeling skin of the world's most shunned "unclean" people—what if that risky touch serves life? What if life is contagious? What if health is infectious? What if the clean is transmissible? As absurd and upside down as this all may sound, Jesus dared to imagine this alternative vision. He dared to live with this holy imagination.

It is delivered and rescued priestly kingdoms that participate in the life-giving blessing of the God plot. What if life is not about the *survival* of ourselves, our institutions, or our deeply held beliefs? What if life is about persons, institutions, and deeply held beliefs that exist for the sake of and are emptied out on behalf of the diseased, the broken, and the dead for their healing, wholeness, and life?

Just What Is This Different Vision? This Alternative Mind? This Holy Imagination?

What is this *alternative* mind that no longer becomes paralyzed by fear for its survival? What is this *different* vision that enables one to trust the delivering, providing, covenanting God so that the survival tactics of holy hills, sacred cows, or substitute kings are no longer necessary? What is this *holy* imagination that moves one to participate in the priestly, life-giving, blessing-imparting mission of God by daring not only to go to the deathly places but also to participate in and to touch death so that life may take place?

How can we describe this different mind or define this alternative vision? Warning! The discussion that follows is about to introduce what may be the ultimate code word, the cliché of clichés, of the Christian faith! So beware. When the voices—both priestly and prophetic, both Sadducee and Pharisee, gathered around Jesus, they earnestly sought what summed up the mind, the heart, the imagination, of God. In their inquiry of Jesus they really wanted to know more about the mind of Jesus, the imagination and vision that guided his teachings and prompted his unusual activities.

In at least some ways, the question asked of Jesus when the Pharisees and Sadducees came to him in Matthew 22:36 was a trap: "Teacher, which commandment in the law is the greatest?" Would he answer from the "handbook" of the priestly voice, now reflected in the Sadducees, who were in power in the temple? Or would he answer from the "handbook" of the prophetic voice, now corresponding to the Pharisees, who were not in power in the temple but still possessed significant religious authority. Although the Sadducees and Pharisees appear together, you can be certain that they were looking for an answer from Jesus that would side him with one or the other of them.

Although it was a trap, the question was legitimate. The answer to that question would reveal the unique mind-set and holy imagination of Jesus. If he really did reveal the One whom he called Father, it would also reveal the unique mind-set and holy imagination of God. It was now the moment of truth: would he point to the prophetic Deuteronomy, or would he point to the priestly Leviticus? And Jesus responded: "'You shall love the Lord your God with all your heart, and with all your soul, and with all your mind.' This is the greatest and first commandment" (vv. 37-38).

Ah! Deuteronomy wins. The Pharisees had to be elated! Until he continued: "And a second is like it: 'You shall love your neighbor as yourself.' On these two commandments hang all the law [torah, i.e., priestly teaching] and the prophets" (vv. 39-40). That's straight from Leviticus.

Uh-oh! Whose side was Jesus on? Neither. From whose handbook did he quote? Both. Whose mind did he reveal? God's. The answer was in both of their handbooks all along. It was right there in front of them from the start: love—undivided loyalty to God and undivided commitment to one's fellow human being. So in Jesus' words we find a trusting fidelity to God that seeks no survival tactics for security and fertility combined with a life-giving faithfulness to one's neighbor that no longer finds value in clinging to one's own life by hoarding, killing, enslaving, or taking. Thus the mind of Christ is a love that refuses to take in order to survive but rather consistently gives in order that others may live.

Jesus' words concerning love go far beyond a feeling of empathy. As we have seen throughout the God plot, love is ultimately fidelity. It is never abstract; it is always fidelity with hands and feet. If power is the capacity to act upon the life of another, then from the viewpoint of this alternative, holy, mind-set, love must be the ultimate expression of that capacity to act. Love is the ultimate expression of power used for the sake of the other in contrast to power used for the sake of one's own survival. Love is the ultimate capacity to act upon the life of another for the sake of his or her good, for the sake of life, and for the sake of the divine agenda. Love *is* the God plot! Far beyond a sentimental feeling or a strongly held affection, love is the action of extending God's creative life, blessing, and good into the life of another. Love is a synergistic partnership with the life-giving, blessing God.

eleven

IMAGINING THE POSSIBILITIES FOR ALL HUMANITY

AN UNDERLYING conviction has informed all that we have said concerning the God plot: God is actively at work doing something in his world. Far beyond a sacred text within the covers of a book called the Bible, the God plot is ongoing and continues to play itself out right here, right now.

From our observations of the way the God plot unfolds in Scripture, we have discovered that if God's people—his covenant community—are ever to love their covenant God with *all* their *leb* ("heart"/"mind"), then God himself must transform their *leb*. This transformed *leb* or mind-set will so trust and love this covenant God that the addictive practices of clinging to life, hoarding life, and securing life for survival will be abandoned. This transformed mind-set will become incarnate in flesh and blood as the covenant people become synergistic partners in the mission of God, extending life to the most lifeless places.

To imagine a community among the human race with such a transformed *leb* takes us toward the ultimate destination of the God plot. As we begin to imagine what that "called out" people (*ekklēsia* or "church") with transformed, Christlike minds might look like, God's anticipated future for the world begins to burst in upon the community. That community begins to put into flesh and blood actions (i.e., begins to incarnate) a life that is moved and motivated by this transformed way of thinking.

However, if we are to see the God plot to its completion, to its ultimate purpose (Gk., *telos*), our imagination must go even further. For a moment, allow your imagination to expand to even broader, wider, deeper horizons. Let it stretch beyond a single community of people that are "called out" (*ekklēsia*) from the world in order to be a blessing to the world, and let it begin to imagine what that world itself might look like as that community steps back into it. For a moment, allow your imagination to be different, unique, holy. Imagine *all humanity*. Even more, imagine *all creation*! It is with all humanity and all creation that the God plot starts, and it is with all humanity and all creation that the God plot ends. Ultimately, the God plot dares to imagine all humanity at one with God, with each other, and with creation. It dares to imagine humanity reconciled with and restored to an undivided trust in the life-giving, blessing God; reconciled with and restored to both neighbor and enemy; and reconciled with and restored to its proper place in creation.

Scripture opens with a remarkable picture of God's intentions for all humanity. The opening chapters of Scripture depict the divine intentions for the human race in its entirety—all of *'adam* ("humanity") as it faithfully fleshes out its purpose (*telos*) for which God created it. From the beginning, the God plot has not simply been for a unique group of people called ancient Israel or the Christian church. From the beginning, the God plot has been for the human race.

Throughout our journey together, we have especially emphasized the communities in covenant with the Lord—ancient Israel in the Old Testament and the church in the New Testament. This emphasis is quite fitting in any discussion of the God plot. As we have seen, the nonmicromanaging, partnering God has called a unique community into existence to cooperate with him in his creative, life-giving, delivering, providing, and covenant-making life and mission. However, within the story of God, this community, whether ancient Israel or the Christian church, finds itself within a much larger context. Within the God plot, the Lord is committed to the entirety of the human race for the sake of all of his creation. This God is not a parochial deity that chooses certain individuals through the rejection and destruction of the rest of the human race. Neither is this God a provincial deity that seeks the good of humanity alone. His divine vision is wider, deeper, and fuller. He is God of all nations and all people groups to the furthest corners of the globe, as well as of everything else he has made.

As God of all creation, he has pronounced his creative work good and has commissioned humanity to act as caregivers of all he has brought into existence. No wonder when the story of God reaches its grand finale in the book of Revelation—when indeed God's will is carried out on earth just as it is in heaven—John the Revelator would boldly declare with the most inspired imagination possible,

By your blood you ransomed for God saints from every tribe and language and people and nation; you have made them to be a kingdom and priests serving our God, and they will reign on earth. (5:9-11)

The kingdom of the world has become the kingdom of our Lord and of his Messiah, and he will reign forever and ever. (11:15)

See, the home of God is among mortals. He will dwell with them as their God; they will be his peoples, and God himself will be with them. (21:3)

We could have easily begun our discussion of the God plot where Scripture itself begins—the opening chapters of Genesis. Although the covenant people traced their unique identity back to the gracious activity of God's unique deliverance from slavery and provision in the wilderness, there is a much wider, broader, deeper context. It is the context of creation itself.

Back to the Beginning in Order to Imagine the Future

In the opening chapters of Scripture, we discover the most remarkable story of God's ultimate intentions. Over the abyss of darkness and chaotic waters, the life-giving Spirit of God hovers as God begins to carry out those intentions. First opening up the space for life to exist, God proceeds to fill up the space with an abundance of life. "Light, be!" And what God spoke now appeared: "Light became." Evaluating the light as appropriate for serving its divine purpose, God announces, "It is good!" He proceeds to cast light into the abysmal darkness, *dividing* the darkness in half. With the creation and use of the light to divide darkness, the dramatic, creative, room-making, life-giving intentions of God have begun.

"Let there be a firmament" (Gen. 1:6, KJV), God says, and then he casts the firmament into the chaotic waters *dividing* the life-threatening, watery abyss right in two. "Let the land appear and serve as borders for the life-threatening sea." And the room-making, life-giving commitment of God continues. It is quite amazing, isn't it, that this God consistently refrains from micromanaging or coercing his creative intentions from the very start. Light, firmament, land—all instruments to carry out the space-making, life-giving intentions of God. Then God empowers the land to send out trees and herbage and plants of every kind. Later, he will empower that same land to send out animals of every kind just as he empowers the waters to swarm with swimming creatures of every type. This God who has no appetite for power mongering even empowers the sun and the moon to rule over day and night. Filling up the waters above with birds and the waters below with fish, God *blesses* them: "Be fruitful . . . multiply . . . and fill" (v. 22). As we have previously observed, "to bless" (*barak*) is to pronounce life, fertility, and hope upon and into the life of another. To be blessed (*barak*) in order to be a blessing (*berakah*) is to receive life for the sake of becoming a life-giving instrument used by God for another.

With everything in place, God proceeds to demonstrate in the most vivid way imaginable that he will forever refuse to be a coercive, micromanaging force over his creation. No doubt, in the future his covenant people and all of creation will repeatedly declare that the Lord is King. However, from the outset this God clearly demonstrates the manner in which he will exercise his divine kingly power. Refusing to hold tightly to his power with a self-serving clinched fist, he announces, "Let us make humankind [*'adam*] in our image, according to our likeness; and let them have dominion over the fish of the sea, and over the birds of the air, and over the cattle, and over all the wild animals of the earth, and over every creeping thing that creeps upon the earth" (v. 26). He then proceeds to create the human community as his custodian to rule over his creation. No wonder the psalmist would eventually exclaim, "When I look at your heavens, the work of your fingers, the moon and the stars that you have established; what are human beings that you are mindful of them, mortals that you care for them?" (Ps. 8:3-4).

The beautiful poetic statement of Genesis 1:27-28 describes how God carries out his intentions to create a cooperative partner: "So God created humankind in his image [singular], in the image of God he created [it/him] [singular]; male and female he created them [plural]. God blessed them [plural], and God said to them [plural], 'Be fruitful and multiply.'" Similarly, 5:1-2 summarizes God's creative work of human beings: "When God created humankind, he made [it/him] [singular] in the likeness of God. Male and female he created them [plural], and he blessed them [plural] and named them 'Humankind' [*'Adam*] when they [plural] were created." God puts into place a community of human beings who together, in cooperation with God, with fellow humans and with creation itself will "be fruitful and multiply, and fill the earth and subdue it" (1:28).

The story of God's creation of the human race as recounted in Scripture has an extraordinarily image-provoking way of describing the function of the human community. The human race is the *image of God*. What a remarkable way to articulate the human possibility with holy *imag*ination: "to image" this life-giving, power-sharing God of the universe to all creation. The image-bearing function of humanity is to point to the God who brings light to darkness, life to deathliness, deliverance to slavery, provision to hunger. As the *image of God*, the human race carries out its partnering mission with God.

So just what is this "image" of God? Throughout the history of God's people, this question has evoked tremendous debate. Out of this debate, many fascinating, creative, and often good suggestions have been given. Does humanity somehow physically look like God? Does it have the capacity to think in rational ways or perhaps have some type of conscience like God? Is it an indication of the relationship between a human soul and the nature of God? Does the human race create like God? Could it be an indicator of the ultimate immortal nature of humans?

In spite of all of the intriguing suggestions that have been given, it has often been all too easy to overlook how our ancestors who recounted this story would have understood an *image*. We can easily take the concept completely out of the context of the scriptural story itself and let it become a cliché or code word for an abundance of other ideas. Many decades ago, the Old Testament scholar Norman Snaith somewhat humorously suggested that in our theological search for meaning in the concept, well-meaning people have often "lifted the phrase 'the image of God' (*imago Dei*) right out of its context, and, like Humpty-Dumpty, they have made the word mean just what they choose it to mean."[1]

As theologian Karl Barth reflected on suggestions of the meaning of the concept of the *image of God* by some of the great figures of church history, he concluded that "we might easily discuss which of these and the many other similar explanations is the finest or deepest or most serious. What we cannot discuss is which of them is the true explanation of Gen. [1:26f]. For it is obvious that their authors merely found the concept in the text and then proceeded to pure invention in accordance with the requirements of contemporary anthropology."[2]

Rather than being a reference to looking, thinking, or creating like God, and far beyond a reference to a soul-like resemblance or immortality, our ancestors would have had a very clear understanding of the *unique function* or purpose of an image. In other words, the concept of image is especially concerned with purpose or *telos* rather than physical or spiritual representation. An image, accordingly, has a specific vocation or calling.

Just what is this task to which the human race is summoned by God? When our ancestors would have heard the term *image* or would have even seen an image, they would likely have thought in one of three directions. In the first place, they would have been aware of the common practice in the ancient world of kings creating statues or images of themselves and then setting those statues or images up in the middle of their capital cities or in outlying regions (for example, see the image set up by Babylonian King Nebuchadnezzar in Dan. 3:1-7). Throughout history, rulers have constructed these statues or, in other instances, paintings and portraits of themselves in order to be on public display. As the image points away from itself to the one who rules, it functions as a vivid reminder to the inhabitants of the one who ultimately reigns over the territory.

Our biblical ancestors clearly would have understood that upon completion of his creative work, the Lord was indeed King. The Psalms regularly celebrate the kingship of this God who has divided the darkness and the light and has filled it up with signs of his sovereignty. Psalm 93:1-4 celebrates that this Divine Creator King who has overcome the waters will never be overcome by the waters:

> The LORD is king, he is robed in majesty;
>> the LORD is robed, he is girded with strength.
> He has established the world; it shall never be moved;
>> your throne is established from of old;
>> you are from everlasting.
> The floods have lifted up, O LORD,
>> the floods have lifted up their voice;
>> the floods lift up their roaring.
> More majestic than the thunders of mighty waters,
>> more majestic than the waves of the sea,
>> majestic on high is the LORD!

Psalm 97:1-5 similarly celebrates the creaturely response to this divine Creator King:

> The LORD is king! Let the earth rejoice;
>> let the many coastlands be glad!
> Clouds and thick darkness are all around him;
>> righteousness and justice are the foundation of his
>> throne.
> Fire goes before him,
>> and consumes his adversaries on every side.
> His lightnings light up the world;
>> the earth sees and trembles.

The mountains melt like wax before the LORD,

before the Lord of all the earth.

Having divided darkness and chaotic waters, having contained the seas within the boundaries of land, having empowered the land to put forth both plants and animals, having empowered the sun to rule the day and the moon to rule the night, and having filled up the waters above with birds and the waters below with fish, the Lord reigns over this created order and the life within it. As the fitting climax to his divine kingship over his creation, the Divine King rounds out his creation by constructing a statue of himself that will point toward the Creator King.

When speaking of the image of God, our ancestors could very likely have had in mind the statue or image of a conquering king. However, they were also very familiar with another image or statue. Just as across the world today in various religions, each temple in the ancient world was dedicated to a specific deity. Thus each temple would contain an image or idol of the god to whom that temple was dedicated. While the image was not viewed in and of itself as the god per se, it clearly had the task or vocational purpose of identifying the god to whom this temple belonged and to whom the worshipper was to pay homage. Similarly, upon completion of his holy dwelling place on earth, the temple of his creation, the Lord brings his creative work to a crescendo as he places an image of himself in its midst: the human race. The purpose or calling of this image was to point to the One to whom this holy temple of God's creation belongs. Indeed, as the psalmist anticipates entering into the temple of the Lord in Psalm 24:1-2, he declares, "The earth is the LORD's and all that is in it, the world, and those who live in it; for he has founded it on the seas, and established it on the rivers." In the midst of this holy abode of God, the Lord creates and establishes his image to make clear that this temple of creation is his and that he alone is worshipped within it.

Certainly our ancestors would have had familiarity with both the statue of a reigning king and the image of a god within a temple. However, a third understanding is likely to have come to the minds of our biblical ancestors as they made reference to an image. Early in the book of Genesis, the language concerning the birth of Adam and Eve's third son, Seth, is very reminiscent of the creation of humanity in the image and likeness of God. In 5:3 we read that Adam "became the father of a son in his likeness, according to his image, and named him Seth." There was a clear "family resemblance" between the son and his father. Common blood runs through both the father's and the son's veins. One might even say that when you have seen the son, you have seen the father. This is the very language of Jesus regarding his relationship to the Father in John 14:9-11: "Whoever has seen me has seen the Father. How can you say, 'Show us the Father'? Do you not believe that I am in the Father and the Father is in me? The words that I say to you I do not speak on my own; but the Father who dwells in me does his works. Believe me that I am in the Father and the Father is in me." No wonder John would understand Jesus as the Word of God that became flesh, as "the glory as of a father's only son, full of grace and truth" (1:14). No wonder he would say that "no one has ever seen God. It is God the only Son, who is close to the Father's heart, who has made him known" (v. 18). Similarly, it comes as no surprise that the apostle Paul describes Jesus as "the image of the invisible God, the first-born of all creation" (Col. 1:15).

While the language of image can demonstrate the relationship between a king and his statue or between a god and its idol, in both instances the relationship is between a person and an object. To use the language of the Jewish philosopher Martin Buber, both of these relationships are "I-It" relationships. However, the Adam-Seth, parent-child, relationship is one between two persons. It is an "I-Thou" relationship. Statues of kings and idols of gods have no mind of their own; they are inanimate. They simply sit idly by and point toward the king or the deity. However, this is not the case in the parent-child relationship. As the image or likeness of the parent, a child not only indicates who the parent is but also points to the parent by means of a mutual, animate, living relationship with the parent.

Whether our biblical ancestors would have associated the depiction of humanity as the image of God with the statue of a king who reigns over a designated territory, the image of a god who is worshipped within a temple, or a child in relationship to the child's parent, an image consistently points away from itself to the king, the deity, or the parent. The function of the image is never to point back to itself but always to point forward to the one who is being "imaged." To fail to do so is to fail at purpose, vocation, *telos*. Again, the words of the Westminster Shorter Catechism capture the essence of this human vocation: "What is the chief end of man? Man's chief end is to glorify God, and to enjoy him forever."[3] Certainly as the image of the King, the God, and the Father, Jesus knew his sole vocation: "I glorified you on earth by finishing the work that you gave me to do. . . . I have made your name known to those whom you gave me from the world" (John 17:4, 6).

The image-bearing function of the human race should come as no surprise to us as we have journeyed through the God plot. This function is consistent with the vocation of the covenant people as glory bearers. Jesus understood the same vocation for his disciples as he prayed to the Father, "The glory that you have given me I have given them, so that they may be one, as we are one, I in them and you in me" (vv. 22-23). However, in the end or, perhaps we should say, from the beginning, God has not intended for simply one people or community within the entirety of the human race to carry out this *imaging, glory-bearing, priestly kingdom* task. Just as God had called his covenant people to carry his tabernacling glory into the world, he had created humanity in its entirety to be his image, to bear his character to each other and together to bear his character to all of his creation.

No wonder one of the consistent prohibitions for the people of God concerned the formation of images or idols. To create such an image that points to God is to give up the vocation of humanity itself. It is to shirk humankind's function as the sole image of God in his world, the image of the Lord in his creation-temple.

An Image in Relationship

The human race is certainly more than a passive statue. The detailed depiction of humanity in Genesis 2 provides the most remarkably thought-provoking portrait of *how* the human race as the divine image carries out its image-bearing vocation. It does so by means of relationship.

In a quick series of actions, God establishes the relational nature of the human race. Like a potter shapes clay between his fingers, God intimately and carefully forms the dirt of the ground (*'adamah*) into the human (*'adam*). Humans are one with the ground itself. No wonder God will commission humanity to serve (*'ebed*, literally, "to be a servant to") and to carefully guard (*shamar*, "protect, care for") the earth.

However, humanity is more than a lump of clay. As God exhales the divine breath into the lips of the limp lump of clay, the human inhales and is animated to see, to smell, to hear, to touch, to walk, and to communicate. Humanity becomes a living, breathing soul (life force). Taken from God's creation, the human now has the breath of God in it and thus shares intimacy with both creation (the ground itself) and with the Lord of creation.

The relation-building Creator continues to construct his relational image. For the first time in the creation narrative, God pronounces that something is *not* appropriate: "It is not good for the human being to be alone" (2:18, author's translation). Shaping his relational image, God determines to make *a helper as his partner.* The term for "helper" (*'ezer*) is used in other texts to refer to God himself as he walks alongside his people and provides care, protection, assistance, and fellowship. In 1 Samuel 7:12, after the Lord has brought victory, the Israelites establish a memorial stone and testify that the Lord is indeed their Eben-*ezer* ("Rock of Help"). Rather than indicating one who is inferior or one who walks a step behind, the term for "partner" indicates one who corresponds to the other.

The relationship-building continues. God partners with humanity as he empowers the human to give names to the animals shaped from the same ground from which humanity came. While the animals may provide assistance to the human, none of them correspond to the human.

How can an authentic, intimate, and corresponding relationship ever be established for the human? The ground with all of its herbage is not human; animals are not human; indeed, God is not human. The only authentically corresponding helper would be another human. So human was made for human. And the God plot for the first time in Scripture explodes with the first spoken words of humanity—words of authentic, mutual relationship: "[At last!] . . . bone of my bones and flesh of my flesh" (v. 23).

Here is the vision of God for the human race: be fruitful, multiply, fill, subdue (i.e., tame or domesticate), rule over (i.e., take responsibility as overseer), serve, and protect. The vocation of humanity is *image*, and the nature of that image is *relational*. And God saw that it was good; it was *very* good! (see 1:31).

Relational Image--In Crisis!

With little time to celebrate the image-bearing, relational human race, Scripture's narrative of humanity proceeds quickly to recount the great human crisis. The profound dilemma of the divine image-bearing human race will not come as any surprise for us in the light of our journey through the story of God with his covenant people. In fact, our ancestors' dilemma that was embodied through holy hills, sacred cows, and substitute kings was not unique to them at all. Their dilemma is caught up in the broader dilemma of the human race itself.

As we have observed, the image that is humanity exists to point away from itself to the King who overcame the darkness, to the Deity who dwells in the holy temple, to the Parent who gives life and nourishment to the child. The means by which this image will faithfully carry out its vocation is through relationship—a trusting relationship with the God whom it images, a serving and protecting relationship with the creation of which it is a part and from which it came, and a mutual, nonthreatening relationship among the human beings of which it is comprised.

Just as the covenant community struggled with undivided trust in God, so, too, does the human race. "Did God *really* say . . . ?" (see Gen. 3:1). Empowered to image the Creator through its protective rule over God's creative work, humanity becomes consumed with the question: Is this God of life, deliverance, provision, and covenant *really* trustworthy? Can the image perhaps do more than reflect? If the image is to thrive and be fertile or even to survive and simply "hang on," can the image discover its own means to create (or to destroy), to give life (or to take life), to deliver (or to oppress), to provide (or to hoard)?

Because this God is not a micromanaging divine puppeteer, the divine partnership with image-bearing humanity changes into something else. The calling and vocation for humanity to "image" remains the same. However, out of humanity's ever-haunting fear that it will not survive and out of an almost addictive compulsion to prosper and flourish, humanity's relational nature unravels and disintegrates.

Rather than an unadulterated trust in the Lord whom it images, humanity now has a divided trust in God at its best and a complete lack of trust in God at its worst. Humanity now fears and hides from the God it is to image (3:8-10). Rather than serving and guarding the creation to which it is related, it now abuses its authority as all of creation becomes its servant. Head-crushing enmity and thorn-bearing brokenness become the routine interaction of humanity with God's creation (vv. 14-15). Rather than the joyful exclamation of "[At last!] . . . bone of my bones and flesh of my flesh" (2:23), human relationships become characterized by domination, violence, and revenge. Pain-filled labor becomes the rule of survival. The "pain" in childbearing (3:16) and the "toil" (v. 17) in agriculture are actually the same word in the biblical text (*'etseb*). Surviving and thriving for both men and women, for fertility of the ground and fertility of the womb, will mean toilsome, painful labor. One gender exercises self-serving domination over the other (v. 16); brother kills brother (4:8); one who is wounded becomes the murderer of the wounder (v. 23). Indeed, the agonizing exclamation of Cain to God in 4:13-14 graphically depicts the utter breakdown of the relational nature of the image-bearing human race: "My punishment is greater than I can bear! Today you have driven me away from *the soil*, and I shall be hidden *from your face*; I shall be a *fugitive and a wanderer* on the earth, and anyone who meets me may kill me" (emphasis added).

The divine cooperative partnership with the imaging human race continues to spiral downward as violence (*hamas* in the biblical text) and shed blood affects even creation itself. The grand dilemma of the God plot emerges as the image-bearing human race becomes a misrepresentation of the God it is to image. How can violent life takers accurately and appropriately image this blessing, life-giving God? This God is Deliverer, yet his image is oppressor. This God is Provider, yet his image is hoarder. This God is Covenant Maker, yet his image is covenant breaker. Just before the catastrophic flood, the biblical narrative in Genesis 6:5-6, 11 summarizes the divine-human dilemma graphically and realistically: "The LORD saw that the wickedness of humankind was great in the earth, and that every inclination of the thoughts of their hearts [leb, "mind"] was only evil continually. And the LORD was sorry that he had made humankind on the earth, and it grieved [also 'etseb as described above in 3:16-17] him to his heart. . . . Now the earth was corrupt in God's sight, and the earth was filled with violence." Then just when we thought that the purging, cleansing flood would take care of the human dilemma, God concludes, "I will never again curse the ground because of humankind, for the inclination of the human heart is evil from youth" (8:21).

Even after the great deluge, absolutely nothing changes! The human dilemma remains. But obviously, when the rest of us would throw our hands up in the air and give up, the relentless God has just begun. The God plot continues. In the hands of a creative and creating God, the dismal despair of a mistrusting, violent, power-abusing image becomes the opportunity to make all things new. Indeed, the despair becomes the starting point for imagining a new creation.

A Determined Yet "Partnering" God: Living with Holy Imagination

Into this dilemma of the human race, God calls a community—not for the sake of itself but for the sake of humanity and all creation. So he blesses (gives life to) them so that they become his blessing (instruments of divine life giving) to the world. Thus the God plot continues.

The story of the creation of the human race in the opening two chapters of Scripture does not serve simply as a story of "the way it was." It is ultimately a story of the way it will be—the way the Creator has always intended it to be. It is the story of the covenant-making, creating God who is absolutely determined to take his creation and his image toward the divine purpose, its *telos*. The vision of God, the God plot, dares to hope. It dares to imagine that this vocation of divine glory bearing or divine image bearing is not merely the vocation of one individual within a community or of one community within the human race. It audaciously and boldly imagines, hopes, and dreams that God is ultimately calling the human race to appropriately bear the image of this life-giving, blessing, delivering, providing, and covenant-making God.

Let's be honest! The realities of mistrust, abusive and self-serving power, and violent and destructive activities all too easily diffuse and dilute holy imagination. They blind us to what God is ultimately doing in the world. The community set apart to be a kingdom of divine blessing to the world and to all creation all too quickly seeks its own subsistence and fertility through protectionist measures, hoarding, and survival tactics. Even the slightest flicker of imagination that would envision a human race that does not seek its own preservation through mistrust, abusive power, hoarding, war, self-serving economic practices, and genocide is quickly doused with the flood waters of despair and hopelessness. The deepest desire of the prayer that Jesus taught his followers to pray becomes no more than "pie in the sky": "May your kingdom come, may your will be done, on earth just as it is done in heaven" (see Matt. 6:10). The hope-filled vision of Isaiah becomes no more than a fuzzy impossibility that may occur "out there" but not "right here":

The wolf shall live with the lamb,
> the leopard shall lie down with the kid,
the calf and the lion and the fatling together,
> and a little child shall lead them.
The cow and the bear shall graze,
> their young shall lie down together;
> and the lion shall eat straw like the ox.
The nursing child shall play over the hole of the asp,
> and the weaned child shall put its hand on the adder's
> den.
They will not hurt or destroy
> on all my holy mountain;
for the earth will be full of the knowledge of the LORD
> as the waters cover the sea. (Isa. 11:6-9)

Those moments when the people of God lose all sense of the optimism of God's grace call for more than another cliché. Those moments when the dark shadows of human brokenness, hatred, and violence overwhelm the people of God demand something more than a popular catchphrase or religious code word. Those moments call for prophets, poets, singers, and dancers to daringly imagine, to radically hope, and to boldly dream. Those moments call for something *dif-*

ferent from what the dominant voices of the empire tell us. When even the voices of pop religion lose sight of what God is up to and despairingly conclude that halfhearted loyalty to God, survival tactics, and fertility gimmicks are just the way things are always going to be—those moments call for a *different* vision, a *unique* mind, a *transformed* heart—a *holy imagination!*

Into the preflood and postflood announcement that every inclination or imagination of the human heart (*leb*) is only evil continually comes the call of the God plot: by the grace of God, there has arisen a different vision, a different mind, a holy mind, a holy imagination! By the grace of God, may we imagine the possibilities of what God is doing in the world. The God plot is about just that—living with holy imagination!

NOTES

Introduction
1. Ludwig Wittgenstein, *Philosophical Investigations*, trans. G. E. M. Anscombe, 3rd ed. (New York: Macmillan, 1958), 48.

2. Bernhard Anderson, *The Unfolding Drama of the Bible*, 4th ed. (Minneapolis: Augsburg Fortress Press, 2006), 15.

Chapter 2
1. Søren Kierkegaard, *Purity of Heart Is to Will One Thing* (New York City: Harper TorchBooks, 1956).

Chapter 3
1. Terence Fretheim, *God and World in the Old Testament: A Relational Theology of Creation* (Nashville: Abingdon Press, 2005), 74.

2. Walter Brueggemann, *Peace* (St. Louis: Chalice Press, 2001), 155.

Chapter 4
1. Elvina M. Hall, "Jesus Paid It All," in *Sing to the Lord* (Kansas City: Lillenas Publishing Company, 1993), no. 218.

Chapter 6
1. Rudolf Otto, *The Idea of the Holy* (Oxford, UK: Oxford University Press, 1958), 12-30.

Chapter 8
1. "Westminster Shorter Catechism," in *The Westminster Confession of Faith and Catechisms* (Lawrenceville, GA: Christian Education and Publications Committee of the Presbyterian Church in America, 2007), 355.

Chapter 9
1. Richard Foster, *Celebration of Discipline: The Path to Spiritual Growth, 20th Anniversary Edition* (New York: HarperCollins Publishers, 1998), 7.

Chapter 11

1. Norman Snaith, "The Image of God," *Expository Times* 86 (October 1974–September 1975): 24.

2. Karl Barth, *Church Dogmatics*, vol. 3, no. 1, *The Doctrine of Creation* (Edinburgh: T and T Clark, 1958), 192-93.

3. "Westminster Shorter Catechism," in *Westminster Confession of Faith and Catechisms*, 355.